OLD TESTAMENT
CHALLENGE 1

CREATING
A NEW
COMMUNITY

OTC ⦿LD TESTAMENT **CHALLENGE** 1

CREATING A NEW COMMUNITY

LIFE-CHANGING STORIES FROM THE PENTATEUCH

ĴOHNORTBERG
WITH KEVIN&SHERRY HARNEY

ZONDERVAN™

GRAND RAPIDS, MICHIGAN 49530 USA

WILLOW CREEK RESOURCES

We want to hear from you. Please send your comments about this book to us in care of zreview@zondervan.com. Thank you.

ZONDERVAN™

Old Testament Challenge: Creating a New Community—Discussion Guide
Copyright © 2003 by Willow Creek Association

Requests for information should be addressed to:
Zondervan, *Grand Rapids, Michigan 49530*

ISBN 0-310-24893-0

Interior design by Sharon VanLoozenoord

Interior composition by Beth Shagene

Printed in the United States of America

04 05 06 07 08 09 /❖ DC/ 10 9 8 7 6 5 4

CONTENTS

introduction

Our hearts hunger for order in the chaos of this life. We long for connectedness and community with other people. We thirst to know the God who made us. We strain to hear God speak so that we can discover the purpose of our years on this earth. There is something inside each of us that yearns for a fresh understanding of God, the world around us, and our relationships with others.

So much of life reveals our desire to find order in the midst of chaos. Every time we look around our home and try to figure out how we can clean, straighten, organize, or remodel so that things feel less chaotic, we get a glimpse of this need. Entire companies exist to help us bring order to our schedules, and they make millions of dollars each year as we purchase our day timers, palm-held computer organizers, and personal organizational systems. Bookshelves are filled with resources to bring order to chaotic marriages, families, and friendships. Seminars are held to help people make sense of personal financial lives that have spun out of control. There is something deep inside the human spirit that craves the order that only God can bring.

Into the ancient chaos of the universe, God spoke and brought meaning and order. This same God longs to speak and bring peace into chaotic lives and hearts today. God is the Creator of the heavens and the earth. He is the ultimate authority on bringing form in the midst of chaos. The Bible begins with these words:

> In the beginning God created the heavens and the earth. Now the earth was formless and empty, darkness was over the surface of the deep, and the Spirit of God was hovering over the waters.
> And God said, "Let there be light," and there was light. God saw that the light was good, and he separated the light from the darkness. God called the light "day," and the darkness he called "night." And there was evening, and there was morning—the first day. (Genesis 1:1–5)

The first five books of the Bible, commonly called the Pentateuch, are a revelation of God's creative power. From Genesis to Deuteronomy we watch as God creates the heavens, the earth, animals, human beings, a new community, and a nation of people to follow him. Yet, as God created and brought order, human beings rebelled over and over again and found themselves spinning downward into the chaotic abyss of sin. In response, over and over again, we read of how God came to rescue them and bring form, shape, and meaning to their lives.

If your heart longs to make sense of life, this small group study is for you. The first five books of the Bible answer some of the deepest questions we carry in our hearts. The Pentateuch helps us make sense of life and brings order into the chaos all of us face. In this study we will answer these questions and more:

- What is God's dream for his people?
- What breaks down our human relationships, and what can we do to build them up?
- What kind of a relationship does God want to have with me?
- Is God really with me, and if he is, how can I experience his presence?
- Does God still have power to save and deliver us in our times of need?
- What moral boundaries and structure has God put in place to help us find order in the moral chaos of our day and age?
- How can I learn to follow God more closely?
- How can I draw near to God and experience an intimate relationship with him?
- Does God still speak in a way that is relevant for people today?

As you enter this study of the Pentateuch, do so with an expectant heart. The same God who brought light into the darkness can bring rich new meaning to your life. The Almighty Creator, who made the heavens and the earth, wants to give new hope to your heart. Simply ask him to do his creative, life-changing work one more time, and watch what he does!

God's Greatest Dream

SESSION 1: GENESIS 1 AND 2

Introduction

Words have power!

The things we say and write can change the course of our lives and even history. Consider some of these famous and history-changing words:

> *I have a dream that one day this nation will rise up and live out the true meaning of its creed: "We hold these truths to be self-evident: that all men are created equal."*
>
> *I have a dream that one day on the red hills of Georgia the sons of former slaves and the sons of former slave owners will be able to sit down together at a table of brotherhood. . . .*
>
> *I have a dream that my four children will one day live in a nation where they will not be judged by the color of their skin but by the content of their character.* **MARTIN LUTHER KING**
> (August 28, 1963, on the steps of the Lincoln Memorial)

> *Even though large tracts of Europe and many old and famous States have fallen or may fall into the grip of the Gestapo and all the odious apparatus of Nazi rule, we shall not flag or fail. We shall go on to the end, we shall fight in France, we shall fight on the seas and oceans, we shall fight with growing confidence and growing strength in the air, we shall defend our Island, whatever the cost may be, we shall fight on the beaches, we shall fight on the landing grounds, we shall fight in the fields and in the streets, we shall fight in the hills; we shall never surrender.* **WINSTON CHURCHILL**
> (June 4, 1940, in the British House of Commons)

> *I am the way and the truth and the life. No one comes to the Father except through me.* **JESUS CHRIST**
> (John 14:6)

Just as these words had a radical impact on the course of history, so the opening chapters of Genesis introduced words that changed history. The beginning words and themes of Genesis are more countercultural than most of us have ever dreamed.

Looking at Life

1 Describe a time when the words someone wrote or spoke had a dramatic impact on your life.

Learning from the Word
Read: Genesis 1

2 How does Genesis 1 challenge the prevailing worldview of the people who first read these words (as defined in the sidebar "The Way Things Were")?

3 What insights do you gain about the character of God from Genesis 1?

How do you see the distinct persons of the Trinity (Father, Son, and Holy Spirit) working in harmonious partnership in the opening three verses of the Bible?

Read: Genesis 2:15–25

In light of Genesis 1 and 2:15–25, how does God feel about his creation in general and human beings in specific?

$\boxed{4}$

How does your perspective on human beings compare with God's?

In light of God's view of human beings, respond to *one* of the following questions:

$\boxed{5}$

- *How will you be changing a behavior pattern toward one of your family members?*

- *What will you be doing differently in how you relate to a person at work or school?*

- *How will your attitude and behavior change as you relate to a person you don't tend to get along with?*

What do these opening chapters of Genesis teach you about the relationship between the creation and the Creator?

$\boxed{6}$

7 Tell about a time when you experienced God's presence and power while in his creation.

How did the beauty and majesty of God's creation move you to give praise to the Creator?

8 Give an example of how we can fall in love with the things of this earth and how they can become more important than God, the one who made them.

9 How can an excessive passion for material things break down our community with God?

Describe a time when you saw this happen in your life.

How can an excessive love of material things erode our community with one another?

10

What do you do to battle against this happening in your life?

The temptation to love the things of this world is illustrated in a painfully clear manner in a magazine ad for a particular car company. The marketing team came up with this slogan:

*"You can't buy happiness,
but now you can lease it!"*

Genesis gives us a new perspective. We can't buy it, we can't lease it, but God invites us to freely receive what we could never afford.

Closing Reflection

Take a few minutes of silence for personal reflection . . .

In this portion of the Old Testament, and throughout the Bible, we are taught that it is easy for us to give our devotion to the things of this world and forget the One who made them and gave them to us. Identify one material thing that can get too strong of a grip on your heart. It might be a certain food, an entertainment or hobby you enjoy, or the pursuit of some new material thing. Offer this to the Lord. Ask him to help you have a new perspective on this as a gift from his hand and not an end in itself.

You might even want to abstain from a certain food for a week, or give up a hobby or entertainment for a month. Find some creative way to get your eyes off the things of this world and back on the giver of all good gifts.

Take time to respond to these closing questions:

> *What challenge did God place on your heart during your time of personal reflection? How can your small group members pray for you and keep you accountable to grow in this area of your life?*

Close your small group by praying together . . .

- Pray for eyes to see the beauty and wonder of God's creation.

- Pray for discipline as you seek to keep God first in your life above all other things.

Old Testament Life Challenge

Take time in the coming week to go for a walk with your Creator. Set aside no less than fifteen minutes for this experience. As you walk, imagine God, the Creator of heaven and earth, walking beside you. Be sure to let him know what you think of his creation. What do you see that is "very good"? Pay attention to things you hear, smell, feel, and encounter that help you give praise to him. Let him know that you see his fingerprints all over creation.

To solidify your encounter, you could record this experience in some creative way. Write a journal entry, compose a song or poem, draw a picture, or find some other way to express how you have experienced the beauty of the Creator through the artwork of creation.

Community Busters

Introduction

As you begin this small group study, ask for four volunteers from your group. Have three members sit close together in chairs (all facing inward toward each other). It would be good to have the rest of your small group members sitting a little ways back in a circle around these three. These three chairs and people are going to represent the Trinity.

Remember, the members of the Trinity (God the Father, God the Son, and God the Holy Spirit) are in perfect community. There is no division, no conflict, and no sin. There is only perfect love, joy, and community.

Now, place a chair in the middle of the three chairs that are already occupied by your small group members. Have your fourth volunteer sit in this chair. This person symbolizes human beings (at this point Adam and Eve), who have been invited to join in the community, love, and joy of the Trinity. Take a moment and look at this amazing picture. What a staggering reality—God has invited us into relationship with himself!

Now, have a member of your small group read Genesis 3:1–12.

After you have read this, ask the person in the middle of the circle to stand (representing human beings before God).

Have a group member (one of the three sitting on the chairs) read Genesis 3:13–20.

After you have read this, ask the person in the middle of the three chairs to move out of the circle and set his or her chair outside the circle. If you know which direction is east, have that person move this direction.

Have a group member (one of the three sitting on the chairs) read Genesis 3:21–24.

While everyone is still in his or her place after this brief dramatic reading, invite a group member to offer up this prayer:

> We come before you today, Father, Son, and Holy Spirit, and we celebrate the perfect community you represent. We come confessing that we know more about broken community than we do about wholeness and harmony. But we also come confessing that we long to find our way back into perfect community with you and with each other. We know the loneliness and pain of being on the outside and pray you will show us the way home. Amen.

Invite all your group members to find regular seats as you continue your time together.

Looking at Life

Describe a time you felt on the outside of some social circle or some group of people and tell how this experience impacted you.

1

Tell about a time you felt accepted, loved, and included. Describe how this made you feel.

2

Learning from the Word
Read Genesis 3:1–5; 1 Peter 5:8–9; James 4:7; and John 8:44

A LOOK AT THE SERPENT'S TACTICS
The enemy comes into the picture early in human history! He is not called Satan in this story, but the Christian church came to identify the serpent with the evil one (see Revelation 12:9). The Genesis account gives us a brilliant exposition of how temptation works. This was true at the beginning of time, and it is just as true today!

Satan twists the truth! He begins with a lie. He twists the truth and misquotes God. Had God said Adam and Eve could not eat from any tree at all? No. God said they could eat from *every tree* except one. In Genesis 2:9, we are told that there were all sorts of trees that were beautiful to see and that their fruit was delicious to eat. Adam and Eve were invited to feast on the fruit of all of them, except for one.

Satan wants us to see God as more severe than he really is. Satan misquotes God in an effort to plant a doubt in the woman's mind. He wants her to doubt the goodness of God. He wants her to think, *I can't trust that God has my best interests at heart. I think if I really obey God fully, I will miss out on something good, so I guess I will have to watch out for myself in this world.* The decision to sin always involves these kinds of thoughts. When speaking to the serpent of the forbidden fruit, Eve adds the words, "and you must not *touch it*." God never said, "You must not touch it." But

17

in Eve's mind, she's making God a little more severe than he really is. She's making him a little unreasonable *so that disobeying him becomes more justifiable*.

Satan attacks our vulnerable spots and isolates us from community. As Eve is engaged in her process of deliberation and dealing with temptation, she does not involve the man. When we play with temptation and do it in isolation, we are in grave danger. The enemy wants us to keep it to ourselves—to keep things hidden in the dark of our own heart. But when we don't tell anybody else about our struggle and temptation, we make ourselves infinitely more vulnerable.

> The first step on the way to victory is to recognize the enemy.
>
> **CORRIE TEN BOOM**

Satan wants us to fixate on sin. As Eve looks at the forbidden fruit, she becomes obsessed with it. She keeps thinking about what she will miss if she doesn't eat it. She keeps looking at it, obsessing over it without God or another person to challenge her thinking. And when she does that, the next step becomes inevitable.

Satan entices us to invite others into our sin. When we read the account of sin entering the world, we simply read that Eve gave Adam some of the fruit, and he ate. Have you ever noticed that sin loves company? So often, when a person enters into sin, they want others to join with them. Just as misery loves company, sin loves to invite others to take a taste.

---

3 In our day, Satan tends to be portrayed in two very different ways. Sometimes he is pictured as a cartoon character with little horns, a tail, and a red suit. No one takes this guy seriously. On the other end of the continuum, Satan is pictured as an unstoppable force of evil that Christians have no hope of resisting. What do these passages teach you about the real character and tactics of Satan?

How do these passages paint a picture of the enemy that contradicts those we see in the media?

How do you see Satan using these same tactics in the world today?   **4**

> To be in subjection to the desires of the flesh, and to yield to them, is the most extreme form of slavery. To keep those desires in subjection is the only true liberty.
>
> **CLEMENT OF ALEXANDRIA**
> (second century)

Which of the various tactics of the devil do you find easiest to resist and which do you find the most difficult to resist?   **5**

What helps you resist the temptations of the enemy?

6

Respond to *one* of the following questions:

- *Describe a time you began to doubt God's goodness toward you and tell how this doubting impacted your life.*

- *Satan tries to get us to see God as more severe than he really is. Tell about a time you resisted the temptation Satan put in front of you because you were deeply aware of God's goodness.*

- *If you were the devil and were going to plan an offensive against you, where would you mount your attack? What can you do to fortify this area of your life so the enemy can't get to you as easily?*

- *Why do we tend to run from community when we are struggling with sin, and what are some of the consequences we face when we do this?*

- *What are some ways you have discovered that help you turn your eyes away from temptations?*

Read Genesis 3:6–24

THE CONSEQUENCES OF SIN

We would love to think that our sins bear no consequences. As a matter of fact, when our hearts grow particularly dark, we can even convince ourselves that our sins cause no pain to anyone, even ourselves! Yet we all know this is simply not true. Genesis chronicles the extensive damage that comes from sin. There are consequences!

When Adam and Eve sinned, we immediately see the consequences. Their eyes are opened. That, of course, is what they were hoping would happen. But what a nightmare they see. They look at each other, and the beauty of the image of God—the *imago Dei*—has been horribly twisted and marred.

Adam and Eve also discover the reality of shame. When they look at each other, they see a stranger. They want to hide. For the first time, they are ashamed. The consequences of sin are horrific. Adam and Eve are alienated from themselves, alienated from each other, alienated from their God, alienated from their work, and alienated from creation. Before, they walked with God in the cool of the garden. Now, when he comes to walk with them, they run away!

When God asks Adam where he is, Adam makes an amazing statement. He tells God that he is afraid and is hiding. Wow! This is the first mention of fear in the Bible. Sin creates fear in our hearts and drives us away from the very One, the only One, who can remove the pain and consequences of our sin.

Then God confronts Adam and asks him if he has broken the commandment and eaten fruit from the tree that was clearly off limits. When facing this direct and incriminating question, Adam carefully reflects on the importance of taking personal responsibility for his actions. He summons up all of his courage and says, "The woman *you* put with me. She wasn't my idea. She is at fault!"

The moment Adam and Eve disobey God and eat the fruit, death begins to set in around them. Certainly physical death begins, but the consequences of sin are deeper and wider. The woman is told she will face pain (labor) in her delivery of children. The man is told he will experience pain (labor) in his work. In the Hebrew, the language gives the sense that the curse is similar for both the man and the woman—pain has entered into the human experience.

7

The moment Adam and Eve took and ate from the tree, there was a seismic shift! Pick *one* of the following areas and describe what changed:

- *Their relationship with each other*
- *Their relationship with God*
- *Their emotional state and how they saw the world*
- *Their spiritual state and how God saw them*

How are we still feeling the aftershocks of how sin has impacted this area of life?

8

God spoke a curse on the serpent, Eve, and Adam (Genesis 3:14–19). What price would each of them pay for their sin? How is the human family still living under these curses?

Adam and Eve hid from God. They ran away because of their sin and shame. What are some of the ways we tend to run from God when we are struggling with sin?

9

What are some of the possible consequences when we run from God in the face of facing temptation?

10

What would running toward God in the face of temptation look like in your life?

Three steps into sin
1. Contemplation
2. Rationalization
3. Consent
P.S. Sin always affects others.

RUTH BELL GRAHAM

Closing Reflection

Take a few minutes of silence for personal reflection . . .

What is the main area in which you are under attack today? How are you doing in your efforts to resist temptation and honor God in this area of your life? Quiet your heart and invite the Holy Spirit to uncover any hidden area of sin and temptation. As you sense God speaking to you, take time to confess any area you have been giving in to the temptations of the enemy.

Take time to respond to this closing question:

> *How can your small group members stand by your side and fortify*
> *you as you seek to resist the enemy in a specific area of temptation?*

Close your small group by praying together. Move in two different directions as you close in prayer:

- Lift up prayers of thanksgiving for the power God gives in Jesus Christ to resist and overcome temptation. Be sure to express specific thanks for ways God has delivered you.

- Offer prayers from small group members, and for yourself, to be able to resist the temptations we all face on a regular basis.

Old Testament Life Challenges

A NOTE OF GRACE

There is a beautiful grace note in this passage. Adam and Eve are naked, both physically and spiritually. Yet God makes garments of skin for his children. Adam and Eve have been running around in stitched fig leaves, and they look severely fashion-challenged. So God becomes a tailor and clothes them so they can come into his presence without being overwhelmed by shame. What a picture on God's grace and love!

If we look closely, we see there is even more going on here. Because the coverings God gave them are made of skin, a sacrifice has been made. For the first time in history, innocent blood has been shed so that human shame might be covered and fellowship with God restored. God is setting the stage for the Passover and, later, the death of Jesus as the sacrifice for our sins. What a powerful reminder of God's grace in these opening pages of the Bible.

Take time this week to read Genesis 3:21; Exodus 12:1–13; and Hebrews 9:15–22. Spend time thanking God for the price he paid to cover your shame and bring you back into right relationship with him.

TIME TO RESIST

Take time this week to memorize a short but powerful verse from the Bible.

As you meditate on this verse, be reminded of two simple realities. First, as you draw near to God, he will come near to you and grant you power and strength. Second, when you stand against the devil, he will run. God's power in you is greater than you can imagine!

Submit yourselves, then, to God. Resist the devil, and he will flee from you.

JAMES 4:7

It's Time to DTR (Define the Relationship)

SESSION 3: GENESIS 12–22

Introduction

Bob and Barb have been dating since their sophomore year of high school. They are now juniors in college. Their relationship has been healthy, and neither of them has ever even talked about dating anyone else. The problem is, Barb is wondering where they are headed. Her heart is growing deeper in love with Bob, and she is starting to think about things like engagement rings, wedding bells, and names for children. Bob clearly loves Barb but never talks about the future or the next steps they might take in their relationship to move to the "next level."

Then one day, Barb calls Bob and tells him it is time for a DTR. She wants to sit down and "Define the Relationship." She needs clarity. She wants to know where they are headed. Barb is wondering if she should start looking for a wedding dress or another man!

DTR moments are common in all of our lives. These are the times when two people need to sit down and clarify where they are going. Couples who have dated for a long time will often hit the point when they need to define the relationship. It can happen in business when someone has been working hard for a company and finally has to ask, "Do I have a future here? Is there room for me to advance? Or should I look for another job?" DTR moments can come in our spiritual lives when God brings us to a place where we have to decide if we are going to follow his leading or do our own thing. We all face moments like this, and the way we respond can impact the rest of our lives.

Looking at Life

1

Tell about how a DTR moment with another person impacted your life.

Learning from the Word
Read: Genesis 12:1–9

DTR 1: THE CALL TO LEAVE (TRAVELING WITHOUT A MAP)

God tells Abraham: "Leave your country, your people and your father's household and go. . . ." Go where? "Go to the land I will show you." Let's be honest, these instructions are a little vague! There is not much here for Abraham to tell Sarah. And, as many of us know, wives like to have details about these sorts of things.

Imagine the conversation they must have had. And remember, these are real people. Just think of what this interaction would have sounded like. "Sarah, pack up all our belongings. We're moving away from everyone and everything familiar to us."

"Where are we going?"

"I don't know exactly. I'll know it when I see it."

You have to believe Sarah would have asked what any wife would ask: "How will we know if we get lost? Whom will we ask for directions?"

Abraham replies, "We won't get lost. God will tell me when we get there."

"God who?" Remember, Sarah didn't know this God.

"I didn't catch his last name."

This would be the only trip in human history when a wife would say, "Where in the world are we?" and her husband would say, "God only knows," and he'd be speaking literal truth!

What were some of the things God called Abraham to leave at this decisive DTR moment of his life, and what would Abraham lose if he obeyed?

2

What did God promise Abraham he would gain if he obeyed and left his old life behind?

3 Tell about a DTR moment when you said "Yes" to God, and report how this decision has impacted your life.

How might your life be different if you had said "No" to God?

4 What is one material thing, relationship, habit, or attitude you know God wants you to leave behind?

How can your small group members pray for you and support you as you seek to follow God and leave this behind?

Read: Genesis 15:1–21

DTR 2: THE CUTTING OF A COVENANT

A *covenant* is "a means to establish a binding relationship where none existed before based on faithfulness to a solemn vow." Faithfulness is the core virtue of covenant behavior. In the Old Testament we find references to "covenant" 285 times. As you read the Old Testament, you cannot help but note that God is the God of the covenant. He is characterized by covenantal love. Sometimes this is referred to as "steadfast love." The covenant term *steadfast love* reminds us that God is the One who makes promises out of the depth of his love. He is also the One who always keeps his promises.

In Genesis 15:18 we read, "The LORD made a covenant." But in the Hebrew it literally means, "The LORD *cut* a covenant." The reason this term was used is both shocking and powerful! In those days, when people made a covenant, they took animals, literally cut them in two pieces, and set the two pieces next to each other, side by side. Then the two parties went for a covenant walk, passing between the pieces of the animal. The symbolic meaning of this walk was, "May this be my fate if I don't live up to the covenant, if I don't honor the covenant, if I am not faithful." Jeremiah 34:18 says, "Those who have violated my covenant, I will treat like the calf they cut in two and then walked between its pieces." When people cut a covenant, blood was shed. It was a way of saying, "I take this very seriously."

As we study God's covenant with Abraham, we need to notice who makes the covenant walk (Genesis 15:17). It is God! God is the One who passes between the dead carcasses of the animals, as if to say, "I will keep my agreement with you, and if I don't, may I be like these animals!" That's unbelievable. God condescends to take an oath. "Abram, I want so much for you to trust me, I'll take the covenant walk. May it be so with me if I don't keep my word to you." This is truly amazing!

In Genesis 15 we discover that Abraham has a broken heart over something very specific. Why is Abraham brokenhearted and why does he feel so deeply about it?

5

6

How does God respond to Abraham's honest expression of personal pain?

7

The process of "cutting a covenant" was bloody and a powerful visual reminder of the cost of establishing a binding relationship. How does the cross of Jesus stand as a similar reminder of the cost that was paid so we can be in covenantal relationship with our heavenly Father?

Read: Genesis 22:1–18

DTR 3: A CALL TO DEEPER FAITH

Genesis 22:1 is a very important first sentence. The writer wants us to know what Abraham does not know, that what he will go through is only a test. The writer knows that the strain of this passage will be too intense for readers if they don't understand, in advance, that this is only a test. God is asking Abraham to take a shocking step of faith. "Will you trust me even when you don't understand? Even when it doesn't make sense?" God has no intention of Abraham killing Isaac; this option is never really on the table, but Abraham does not know this, nor does Isaac.

Respond to *one* of the following questions:

8

- What do you learn about the heart of God in this story?
- What do you learn about the growing faith of Abraham in this story?
- How do you think this whole experience impacted the faith of Isaac?

9

God called Abraham to a place of utter willingness to give up what he loved to follow God's leading. Tell about a time when God called you to make a choice between something very important to you and living in obedience to his call.

How has this decision changed your life?

He asks all, but he gives all.
THOMAS R. KELLY

10 God called Abraham to trust him even when it did not make sense. Share with your group about something you believe God is calling you to do that might be difficult to understand.

How can your small group members support you as you seek God's leading in this area of your life?

Closing Reflection

Take a few minutes of silence for personal reflection . . .

Some things in life make sense and some things just seem to baffle us! God's desire to enter a covenant with Abraham (and with us) is one of those things that seems almost beyond comprehension. He has everything and we have so little (and what we have has been given by him). Yet, God initiates an agreement with Abraham, and through him with us. This agreement or covenant reveals the depth of love God has for us as his children. When we enter a covenant relationship with the living God, we face the most significant DTR moment of our lives.

Reflect on the price God has paid for you to enter covenant relationship with him. It was the life of his only Son, the Son he loved, his son Jesus! Unlike Isaac, who was rescued from the altar, Jesus stayed on the cross and died for us! As you think about the price God paid to show his love for you, begin praying about what you can do to show your love for him.

Take time to respond to this closing question:

*What can we do to show our love and thankfulness to God
for all he has given to us?*

Close your small group by praying together . . .

- Thank God for giving his only Son to establish a covenant relationship with you.

- Pray for a responsive heart when God brings you to DTR moments in your relationship with him.

- Pray for your small group members who shared about an area of their life where they know God wants to bring change.

Old Testament Life Challenges

BLESSED TO BE A BLESSING
God's intention was to be with Abraham in such a profound way that countless people would be blessed through Abraham's life. Abraham was "blessed to be a blessing." Take some time to reflect on whether or not the people around you are being blessed because of your life. Take time in the coming week, each day, to identify at least one way you can be a blessing to someone else. It might be something big, or it might be a small act of service, but begin to live in a way that will bring joy and blessing to those around you.

COVENANT ASSESSMENT
Spend some quiet time this week examining your covenant with God. What did God promise you when you became his follower? What promises did you make when you received Jesus as your forgiver and the leader of your life?

- Identify promises God has kept and celebrate these.

- Identify promises you have kept. Then, take time to rejoice! Also, pray for strength to hold fast in these areas of your relationship with God.

- Be honest about commitments you have not kept and promises you have broken. Confess this sin to God and ask for power to live in a new obedience to his will for your life.

God Is with Us

Introduction

As we read through the opening book of the Bible, we discover that God does not always give us commentary on what we read. The good guys don't always have a halo over their head and the bad guys don't have horns. Sometimes the good people make poor choices and enter into sin. At other times a person who seems like the villain ends up doing something that honors God. In movies and books we can usually figure out fairly quickly who the hero is, but in the Pentateuch it can be hard to tell.

Why is this? Why are so many of the pivotal players such a mixture of strength and weakness? Why are so many of the stories in the Old Testament filled with people who seem so human? The reason is that these people are not to be held up as the heroes in the story. Certainly we can learn a great deal from Abraham and Sarah, but they are not the heroes. There is no question that Joseph's life-lessons are there to teach us about faithfulness and endurance, but he is not to be exalted as the final hero in the story. The stories recorded in the Bible are there to point us to the real hero—God.

God is working with real flesh-and-blood people. God knows that these people are living in a terribly fallen world and that sin does unspeakable damage. So God sheds light on what people are really like, but also on what he is like. At the end of the day, we all need to discover that God is the hero and that each of these stories points us toward him.

Looking at Life

1

Tell about one of your heroes from childhood.

As an adult, what would you describe as the characteristics in a person that would make them a hero to you?

Reflect on this statement: Abraham, Joseph, Miriam, Deborah, Gideon, and the other noteworthy characters in the Bible are not the real heroes of the Old Testament. They were never meant to be seen as heroes. In every story and on every page, we are meant to see one true hero—God! How do you see God shining through as the hero in the Bible?

| 2 |

> All God's giants have been weak people who did great things for God because they reckoned on his being with them.
>
> **J. HUDSON TAYLOR**

Learning from the Word
Read: Genesis 24:1–58

GOD CARES ABOUT THE LITTLE STUFF

It is easy to believe God cares about the big things in the world. International crises; the decisions of presidents, kings, and queens; world hunger; and the spread of the gospel—these are the things that must occupy the heart of God. We have no problem being confident that God wants to be involved in the big things that happen in this world.

But what about the little stuff? Is God available to help me with my personal needs? For instance, does God care enough to get involved in helping me figure out the right career? Is he concerned about helping me choose healthy friends? Does God care enough to get involved in the process of helping me find the right person to marry? As we look at the life of Isaac, we discover that God not only cares deeply about the details of our lives, he wants to get intimately involved with us. God is with us in the big things of life, and he is also with us in the little things.

3

Choose *one* of the characters listed below and tell about how this story reveals the care and provision of God in his or her life:

- Eliezer (the servant of Abraham)
- Isaac
- Rebekah

4

Imagine you are Eliezer (Abraham's servant who found a wife for Isaac). Your journey is over and you have returned home with Rebekah. You are lying in your tent and thinking back on your trip to find a wife for Isaac and everything you experienced along the way. What have you learned about prayer?

What have you learned about the character of Abraham's God?

We all have "little things" in life that can seem insignificant and
unimportant. We might even wonder, "Does God really care about
this area of my life?" How does this passage impact the way you see
God's concern about the "little things" of your life?

LEARNING FROM OUR MISTAKES

Some people never seem to learn from their mistakes. Because they refuse
to learn, they are doomed to repeat the same unhealthy behaviors over
and over again. There are also people who do learn from their mistakes.
These people grow in wisdom and avoid all sorts of pain and struggle.
However, there is a third group of people who are wisest of all. These are
the men and women who learn from the mistakes of others. They watch,
listen, and learn. Rather than having to face the consequences of unwise
choices and actions, they see the results of these things in the lives of
others and avoid them at all costs.

The story of Jacob's life is an example of all three of these kinds of
people wrapped into one. Sometimes when we look at Jacob, we see a
man who repeated the same mistakes over and over. At other times, Jacob
learns from his mistakes and grows in maturity as he discovers that God
is with him, even in the hard times. As we walk through Jacob's life, we
see him grow in wisdom and come to a place where he is able to learn
from the mistakes of others and not have to feel pain before he learns
the lessons God wants to teach him. As we study the life of Jacob, we
are invited to a place of wisdom, where we can discover God's desire to
be with us and teach us in every experience of life.

Read: Genesis 27:1–46

6

By the end of this story, Esau is filled with anger and is ready to kill his brother Jacob. The family tensions have risen to such an intense level that Jacob has to run away to another country. Imagine that a neighbor of this family asked this innocent question, "What happened to Jacob? Where did he go, and why did he leave home?" How do you think *one* of the following people would respond?

- Esau
- Isaac
- Rebekah

Read: Genesis 32

7

Jacob's return home to see his brother comes many years after he ran away for his life. He has married (twice) and has raised a large family during this time. Genesis 32 tells the story of Jacob's preparation to see his brother for the first time in many years. How has Jacob changed during his years away from home?

How is Jacob changed because of his encounter with God (32:22–32)?

Read: Genesis 33:1–11

How has God been with Jacob (Israel) and Esau through their lives?

8

WHEN IS GOD WITH US?

It is easy to recognize the presence of God in our lives when things are going well. When the sun is shining, there is money in the bank account, and our body feels healthy, there is a sense that God is near. But what about on the cloudy days, when the stock market does poorly, the doctor brings bad news, and relationships seem to be coming apart at the seams? Where is God when pain and sorrow envelop our lives? From Joseph we learn that God is still with us, even in the times of greatest darkness. Sometimes we find that God is with us in these times most of all.

Joseph's life seemed to be a series of one loss after another. He was hated by his brothers, who finally sold him as a slave to some travelers heading to Egypt. Once in Egypt, Joseph was sold again. His new master experienced great blessing and gave Joseph freedom to run his household. Before he knew it, his master's wife was making advances on Joseph, and he had to actively resist her. Eventually, she lied and said Joseph had attacked her, and she had him thrown in jail. While in jail, Joseph again experienced the presence and blessing of God. But when he interpreted the dreams of two prisoners and the dreams came true, he was forgotten again. One prisoner promised to remember Joseph when he got out of jail, but he forgot for two entire years! Through all this time, Joseph remained faithful and experienced the presence of God.

Read: Genesis 39:3, 21–23; 50:19–21

How have you experienced God's presence with you during a painful or difficult time?

9

10 What is one difficult situation you are facing in your life right now?

How can your small-group members support you and extend the loving presence of God's care to you during this time?

> God's love is more concerned with the development of a person's character than with the promotion of his or her comfort.
>
> J. IRELAND HASLER

Closing Reflection

Take a few minutes of silence for personal reflection . . .

The writer of Genesis is saying something unprecedented. This had never been said before in the history of the human race. Genesis is teaching us that the one and only transcendent God, who existed before time, who was in the beginning, who created the heavens and the earth, is also the God who is with us right here, right now. In the Joseph story we discover that the Creator of heaven and earth is concerned about people like Isaac, Jacob, Joseph—and us!

Reflect on the many ways God has been with you through your life. Thank God for being with you, in the good times and in the difficult times.

Take time to respond to this closing question:

What are some of the things in life that remind you of God's presence?

Close your small group by praying together.

- Thank God for the ways he has been with you and other small-group members.

- Ask God to show his tender presence in the lives of your small-group members in areas they have asked for prayer.

Old Testament Life Challenges

PRAYER JOURNAL

Too often we offer up vague prayers. In many cases, our prayers are so general that we have no idea whether they are actually answered. It can be a faith-building experience to get specific in our prayer requests. There is no guarantee that every prayer we lift up will be answered in the affirmative. But when a prayer is answered, we can learn to recognize it because the request is specific.

In this study we learned about Eliezer, a man who lifted up a specific prayer that led to a specific answer. Take time in the coming week to start a prayer journal. Use this list at least once a week to record specific prayers. Also, use it to review past prayers and see when God has given specific answers.

A GOD HUNT

To experience God's presence in deeper ways, go on a *God hunt*. A God hunt is simply learning to look for signs that the God who walked with Adam and Eve, Enoch and Noah, Abraham and Isaac, and Jacob and Joseph really is with us. Here are some things you can look for. All of these come from the life experiences of the three men you studied in this session:

1. Concrete answers to specific prayers

2. Leadings or promptings from God

3. Experiencing God's presence in hard times

God the Deliverer

Introduction

Everyone faces moments in life when they need some help. Sometimes we humbly accept a hand. At other times we stubbornly insist on doing things ourselves. Like the person driving late at night who is hopelessly lost, we refuse to stop and ask for directions. We would rather stay lost than admit we need help. We have the strangest ability to live in the worst of situations and pretend everything is under control. Life goes so much better when we can be humble enough to admit when we need help.

The people of Israel came to this place often. They hit moments when they were clearly lost and wandering without direction. There were many times the people of Israel were in trouble but still resisted calling out to God. There were even times God reached out to give them help and direction, but they stubbornly refused his offer of deliverance. When they did this, they often had to live with the consequences. At other times they would cry out and accept God's help when he came to deliver them.

As we look at the history of God's people in the Pentateuch, we are invited to learn from their example. Sometimes they are a positive example of calling on God, hearing his voice, and following his leading. When they do this, they experience heavenly power and deliverance. At other times they are poor examples. We see them trying to make it through the journey of life without asking for directions. When this happens, they find themselves wandering in bondage. The key for us is to learn to follow their good example and to avoid any poor patterns we see in their lives.

Looking at Life

When it comes to driving, there are two kinds of people. First, there are
those who willingly and freely ask directions when they think they are
lost. The second are those people who will drive and drive, trying to figure
it out on their own, even when everyone knows they are lost. Which of
these kinds of people best reflects you? Why do you think you respond
this way?

1

If you could talk with God face to face and ask him for direction in an area
of your life, what would you ask him?

2

How would having an answer to this question impact your life?

Learning from the Word
Read: Exodus 1:1–14

A NEW KING IN TOWN

As we begin Exodus, things are looking pretty good for the Israelites. They are being very fruitful and they are multiplying. Then, in Exodus 1:8, things take a turn for the worse. "Then a new king, who did not know about Joseph, came to power in Egypt." There's going to be tension in Exodus from this verse on—tension that will become conflict and then grow to full-blown warfare. This new pharaoh does not care about ancient history and what Joseph did for Egypt four hundred years earlier. He sees all these Israelites as a threat and begins to treat them mercilessly.

On the one hand, God has made this promise, "I'm going to give you a land." On the other hand, the circumstances keep getting more and more desperate. The chances of the promise ever being fulfilled seem more and more remote. The writer lets us know about this tension so that when the people of Israel are finally delivered, there will be no question that God gets the credit.

This section of the Bible helps us gain a new perspective on our lives when our circumstances get desperate and we are facing a potential pharaoh. When we realize that God has the power to deliver his people from the hand of the pharaoh, we have hope that he can deliver us as well. One of the great gifts God gives us in the Bible is reminders. As we look back on these real-life stories of God's faithfulness, we can know that the same God is watching over us today. We can take time to identify the pharaohs we are facing and acknowledge that God is sovereign over them. We don't have to live in fear. We don't have to run and hide. There is no oppression, no fear, no addiction, and no brokenness that is too much for God to conquer.

3

Describe how the political climate (toward God's people) in Egypt changes from the end of the book of Genesis to the beginning of the book of Exodus.

How has the political climate (toward Christians) changed in your country during your lifetime?

If you use the image of the pharaoh in Moses' day to represent someone or something that has you trapped and oppressed, what is one pharaoh you are facing?

4

What practical steps can you take, in God's power, to begin to resist the power of this "pharaoh" in your life?

5

How can your small-group members help you stand against this "pharaoh" in your life?

All I have seen teaches me to trust the Creator for all I have not seen.

RALPH WALDO EMERSON

Read: Exodus 1:15–2:15

THE LAW OF INVERSION

We live in a world where the powerful rule. God, however, has a different vision for how life should work. We might call God's way *the law of inversion*. That is, God turns everything on its head. God exalts humble midwives above the powerful Pharaoh. God uses a stammering, runaway shepherd to lead his people to freedom. God blesses an obedient wife who stands in the gap for her husband, who has refused to hold to the covenant God established. In the days of the Old Testament, as in our days, God reveals his strength in our weakness; he still exalts the humble and humbles those who exalt themselves.

Jesus had a great deal to say about this same law of inversion. He was clear that there is a special place in the heart of God for those who walk humbly and don't seek to exalt themselves. Jesus put it this way:

> *You know that the rulers of the Gentiles lord it over them, and their high officials exercise authority over them. Not so with you. Instead, whoever wants to become great among you must be your servant, and whoever wants to be first must be your slave—just as the Son of Man did not come to be served, but to serve, and to give his life as a ransom for many. (Matthew 20:25–28)*

6

How do you see the "law of inversion" at work in Exodus 1:15–2:15 and throughout the book of Exodus?

The pharaoh mentioned in the Exodus is never mentioned by name. Shiphrah and Puah, however, are recorded in Scripture to be remembered forever for their bravery and courage. Tell about a person in your life whom you will never forget because they have lived with humble courage and integrity.

FIVE OBJECTIONS . . . GOD CAN'T USE ME!

When God chooses to bring his deliverance, he often does it through surprising people and in unconventional ways. One reason God does this is so that it is clear that *God* is the one who saves and delivers, not people. When God came to Moses and called him to be part of the plan to deliver the nation of Israel, Moses had plenty of reasons why he would not be the best choice for this mission.

Moses' *first* objection is, "Who am I?" It is an argument from a feeling of inadequacy. God simply says, "I will be with you." God wants Moses to understand that his own pedigree or power is not the issue, only God's presence.

Second, Moses asks, "Who are you?" This is an argument of authority. Moses knows he willl have to tell others about this God, and he needs to know whom he is dealing with. God's response is short and to the point: "I AM WHO I AM." God reveals the great name Yahweh and tells Moses that he is the eternal God who always is.

Moses then presents his *third* objection. He wonders what he will do if the people will not listen to him. Moses is afraid the people will think he has made the whole thing up. His own authority and integrity could be questioned. Again, God is patient. He asks Moses a question, "What is that in your hand?" Moses replies, "It's a staff." God says, "Throw it down." Moses throws it on the ground, and the text tells us that it becomes a snake. God is saying, "Moses, trust me." God then gives Moses a few other miracles.

Moses is still not ready to sign on. He offers a *fourth* objection. In effect he says, "Speaking is not one of my core competencies." Moses informs God that he does not feel his public-speaking skills are sharp enough for this particular task. But God counters by telling Moses, "Not a problem. I'm in charge of spiritual gifts. I can take care of that. I made your mouth, and I can give you all you need to speak to Pharaoh."

Finally, Moses is out of formal excuses, so he unloads his *fifth* and final effort to get out of this calling. He simply asks God to send someone else.

8

Which of Moses' five objections do you identify with most closely when it comes to God calling you to serve him?

Read: Exodus 7:14–21; 12:1–13, 29–32

TEN PLAGUES AND DELIVERANCE

Now the battle starts. God initiates a series of "plagues" or "mighty acts" on Pharaoh and Egypt. In the first one, the Nile River is turned to blood. This would have deep meaning to the Israelites. Remember, the Nile had been filled with the blood of their infants. It would be significant for them to see God bringing justice for the heartless brutality of the Egyptians. The plagues that follow force Pharaoh to his knees over and over again. Egypt is invaded by frogs, infested with gnats, and swarmed with flies; their cattle die, the bodies of the people are covered with boils, hail destroys their crops, locusts invade, and darkness descends on the land. Yet through all of this, Pharaoh's heart remains as hard as a stone.

Then the final plague comes on the land. The firstborn son in every Egyptian house dies. From the palace to the jail, every firstborn son who is not protected by the blood of the Passover lamb dies. The people of Israel are protected by the blood, and the Egyptians face sorrow on a national scale. At this, finally, Pharaoh lets God's people leave. The nation of Israel packs all they have and begins their journey to the Promised Land.

9

What parallels can you draw between the Passover (Exodus 12:1–13) and what happened when Jesus died on the cross?

10

When the people of God experienced deliverance from Egypt and the oppression of Pharaoh, they sang songs of praise and celebrated (see Exodus 15). What can you do to celebrate God's deliverance in your life?

What can you, as a small group, do to celebrate the deliverance God gives to all who follow him?

Closing Reflection

Take a few minutes of silence for personal reflection . . .

Quietly, in your heart, begin to list the many ways you have experienced the delivering power of God. Meditate on these things and ask God to bring to mind many other ways he has delivered you.

Take time to respond to this closing question:

> *What is one act of God's deliverance that you have forgotten about that God has brought to your mind during this study?*

Close your small group by praying together:

- Thank God for the many times he has delivered you.

- Thank God for his delivering power throughout all history.

- Give praise to God for the way he has shown his power to deliver in the lives of your small-group members.

- Ask God to reveal himself as the One who delivers in specific areas of need that your small-group members are facing today.

Old Testament Life Challenges

THANKS TO SHIPHRAH AND PUAH

We all have people in our lives who have modeled courageous and risk-taking obedience to God. These can be family members, pastors, Sunday school teachers, neighbors, or friends. Take time this week to write a note to a Shiphrah or Puah from your past. Let them know what their example has meant in your life and thank them for being faithful to God.

DEPENDING ON GOD

Once Israel was back in the Promised Land, they had many opportunities to grow in their trust of God. Because they were surrounded by super-powers who were often at war with each other, Israel had to live in constant dependence on God because they were a small people with a modest army surrounded by massive nations with military might.

Followers of Christ today live in a similar situation. In most parts of the world, Christians do not hold the seat of power or control the government. But, like Israel, we are invited to live with utter dependence on God. Our victories don't come by our might or power, but as Zechariah says, by the Spirit of the Lord.

Identify one life situation or circumstance where you do *not* feel powerful and in control. Commit to lay this situation before God in prayer every day for the coming two weeks. Ask for his delivering power and strength to be revealed as you learn to live in day-by-day dependence on God.

God the Lawgiver

SESSION 6: EXODUS 19 AND 20; LEVITICUS 11:44-45

What Is Purity?

Our society has certain standards and laws designed to guard purity. A whole department of our federal government, the Food and Drug Administration, functions as a watchdog for purity. However, their standards of what counts as pure are surprising.

The standards below are drawn from Food and Drug Administration guidelines:

Apple butter: If apple butter averages four or more rodent hairs per 100 grams, or if it averages five or more whole insects, not counting mites or aphids (which are OK with the U.S. government), the FDA will pull it from the shelves. Otherwise, it goes right on your bagel.

Mushrooms: When you get 15 grams of mushrooms, they're OK unless they contain an average of 20 or more maggots of any size.

Fig paste: If there are more than 13 insect heads per 100 grams, the FDA will toss it out. Apparently other insect body parts are OK, but we don't want to have to look at their little insect faces.

Coffee beans: All the caffeine addicts can get a little nervous now. Coffee beans will only be withdrawn from the market if an average of 10 percent or more of them are insect-infected.

When we think that our food supply is protected by our many laws, we had better think again!

Looking at Life

How do you feel about the FDA regulations for purity of your food?

1

How might reading this list affect you on your next trip to the grocery store?

Learning from the Word
Read: Leviticus 11:44–45; Exodus 19:1–9

GOD IS HOLY, AND WE CAN BE HOLY TOO!

All things being equal, we prefer purity. If we can have coffee made from beans that are only 9 percent infested with insects, or coffee that is 100-percent free of insects, we prefer the pure stuff. When it comes to our food and beverages, we are all in favor of purity.

But when it comes to our own lives, we give ourselves a fair amount of latitude. "After all, we're only human," we say as we justify our impurity. We're prepared to put up with a lower standard when it comes to us. The FDA tells us what is pure enough when it comes to our food. We try to do the same with our lives. The problem is that we work on a sliding scale. Our idea of purity is a far cry from God's definition. God is committed to seeing us grow in holiness.

Here is a simple reality that we must all learn to admit: God is perfectly holy, we are not. We are an unholy people, desperately seeking a way to grow in holiness. How do impure people learn to walk in holiness? The answer is: We walk with a God who is holy, and he transforms us. First, he makes us holy through his cleansing power and grace. Second, he teaches us to grow in holiness as we learn to walk in his ways.

The people of Israel learned that growing in holiness is a process that takes a lifetime. As a nation, they learned that the journey toward holiness carries over many generations and centuries.

2 What do you learn about the heart and character of God from these passages?

True faith can no more be without holiness than fire without heat.

JOHN OWEN

God, who is perfectly holy, is coming to a people who are unholy. He could easily judge them, condemn them, or even just ignore them. Instead, he gives a picture of how he sees his relationship to his people. What image does God use in Exodus 19:4, and what does this picture teach you about your relationship with God?

God uses three images in Exodus 19:5–6 (also see 1 Peter 2:9–10) to help us understand what we can become through his power. What does each of these images teach you about who and what God wants you to be?

3

After God speaks to the people of Israel, they give a clear response (Exodus 19:8). What do you learn about the heart condition of God's people at this moment?

4

As you seek to grow in holiness, what is one area of your life you could yield more fully to God today?

WORD STUDY: HOLINESS

Originally, at its root, the word *holy* simply meant *set apart*. This word pointed to things that were reserved for a special use and were not to be touched or used for anything else. Later this word began to point to moral purity, but at the root of the word is the idea of something (or someone) that is set apart.

In the Bible many objects are said to be holy. In Exodus 3:5, when Moses was on this same mountain, God said, "Take off your sandals, for the place where you are standing is holy ground." In this passage the mountain is said to be holy. Sometimes clothing or certain foods are declared holy in the Bible. These things are set apart for special use to God.

PREPARING TO MEET GOD

Imagine for a moment what it would be like for an unholy people to come into the presence of the holy God. If you want to know the people's response to this real-life experience, you will find it in Exodus 20:18–19. When people really encounter God in all his holiness, the first thing that happens is they are overwhelmed and undone by their own sense of sinfulness.

Isaiah 6:5 records a magnificent vision of God in the greatness of his holiness, and we see Isaiah's response, "'Woe to me!' I cried. 'I am ruined! For I am a man of unclean lips, and I live among a people of unclean lips, and my eyes have seen the King, the LORD Almighty.'" In the New Testament, Peter sees the reality of Jesus' power and holiness, and his response is, "Go away from me, Lord! I am a sinful man" (Luke 5:8).

God invites each one of us to come to the mountain and to see him in all his power and glory. We can fall on our faces in the radiating light of his holiness and be overwhelmed with the reality of our sin and his purity. We can be transformed by an Isaiah moment where we cry out, "Woe is me!" These are the moments we stop making excuses, stop rationalizing, and stop defending the indefensible. Yet to draw near to God in all of his holiness, we must prepare ourselves. We must see ourselves as we really are. Only then will we be ready to see God in his glory.

Read: Exodus 19:10–25; 20:18–20

As the people prepared to meet with God in all his holiness, they needed to do certain things in order to get ready.

5

- What preparations were they to make?
- What restrictions were placed on them?
- Why do you think these things were part of their preparation to meet with God?

Imagine you were on Mount Sinai when God revealed himself (Exodus 19:16–22; 20:18–19). How do you think this experience would have shaped your view of God?

6

What are some of the things we can do to prepare ourselves to meet with God when we gather with his people for worship?

7

Tell about a time you felt or sensed the presence of God, and explain how this experience has shaped your view of God.

THREE KINDS OF LAWS: CIVIL, CEREMONIAL, AND MORAL

The Old Testament law can be divided into three general categories.

Some Old Testament laws can be called *civil law*. Because Israel was a country, there were certain laws that had to do with running the government of a country. Things like property rights and sentencing guidelines for the courts fall into this category. Today the people of God are no longer restricted to one nation. We are scattered throughout all the nations. This means the civil laws about the governance of a nation no longer apply to us in the same way.

Another kind of law can be called *ritual* or *ceremonial law*. These are mostly laws about worship, the sacrificial system, or cleanness versus uncleanness. The laws about circumcision are an example of ritual law. In the New Testament the whole sacrificial and ritual system were fulfilled in Christ. He was the ultimate sacrifice and made any continued sacrifices unnecessary. All the sacrificial laws came to an end when Jesus died on the cross and rose again. In the same way, all of the laws about ritual cleansing became null and void when Jesus paid the price for our sins and offered cleansing through his shed blood. Ritual cleansing only pointed to Christ. The sacrificial system pointed to Christ. Since he has come, the ceremonial laws no longer need to be followed.

God's concern for the heart can be seen most clearly in the third category of Old Testament law, which is called *moral law*. The Ten Commandments are a great example of moral laws. Deuteronomy 6:5 ("Love the LORD your God with all your heart and with all your soul and with all your strength") and Leviticus 19:18 ("Love your neighbor as yourself") are also moral laws. These laws apply at all times. They are not ritual laws that have become void through Christ. They are not civil laws that are now replaced by our national civil laws. These are God's moral laws that will always remain.

Read: Exodus 20:1–17

You may want to read this passage in unison as a small group.

8

The Ten Commandments are "moral laws." They fall into the third category discussed above. Choose one of the Ten Commandments and explain how this law applies to and should govern all people, at all times, in all places.

The first four commandments (Exodus 20:2–11) deal with our relationship with God. What are some of the blessings we will experience if we follow these commandments?

9

What consequences might we face if we break them?

> **W**e do not break the Ten Commandments; we only break ourselves against them.
>
> **C. S. LEWIS**

The next six commandments (Exodus 20:12–17) deal with our relationship with each other. What are some of the blessings we will experience if we follow these commandments?

10

What consequences might we face if we break them?

Closing Reflection

Take a few minutes of silence for personal reflection . . .

Before God ever gave the Ten Commandments, he reminded Israel of his loving concern for them: "I carried you on eagles' wings" (Exodus 19:4). God describes his intention and vision for their future with three phrases that they would never forget:

- *"You will be my treasured possession."* This small, insignificant nation really matters to God.

- *"You will be for me a kingdom of priests."* Every person can relate directly to God. They will have access to and a relationship with their Creator.

- *"You will be . . . a holy nation."* God lets them know that they will be a model community, set apart to draw all the peoples of the earth to God.

Take a few moments of silence to reflect on how God has begun to help you see that you are his treasured possession, his priest, and part of a holy nation.

Take time to respond to this closing question . . .

How does God's law give shape and order to our lives, even when we don't notice it?

Close your small group by praying together:

- Lift up prayers of praise for the goodness of God's law.

- Confess ways you have broken God's law, and ask for a broken heart over this sin.

- Ask God to help you and your small-group members to learn to follow God's law joyfully.

Old Testament Life Challenges

BEING PREPARED

Too often we approach God with a very casual attitude. There is a place
for confidence when we draw near to God, and we know that his arms are
wide open to his beloved children. God is the mighty and holy Creator of
heaven and earth. His power is beyond our wildest dreams. But, like the
people of Israel, we must also learn to prepare ourselves to meet with God.
This is particularly true as we think about gathering together in corporate
worship with the community of God's people.

There are many things we can do to prepare ourselves to gather with
God's people and meet with our heavenly Father. Here are just a few ideas:

- Go to worship feeling physically rested. If you go to
  morning services, be sure to get to bed at a reasonable
  time the night before.

- If you drive to church services alone or with others,
  use the time to pray. Pray for the Spirit to move, pray
  for your heart to be soft, pray for those who will be
  leading worship, pray for visitors who might come,
  and pray for anything else that comes to your heart.

- Arrive early enough that you can park, get into the
  building, visit with those you meet, and still sit down
  five or ten minutes before the service begins. Use this
  time to quiet your heart, confess your sins, and tune
  your soul to God's still small voice.

HOW GOD SEES MY HEART

Take time this week to do a heart check. Use the questions below to begin
a process of self-examination:

- Am I driven to follow God's commands out of fear and
  guilt rather than out of a deep awareness of his love?

- What helps me find joy in following God's commands,
  and what makes this a chore?

- As God looks into my heart today, what does he see? Is
  my heart full of love for him, partially full, or running
  dry?

- What can I do to seek a new and fresh filling of God's
  holy presence in my life?

Lessons from the Wilderness

EXODUS 3:7-10; 13:17-22; 15:22-24; 16:6-32;
DEUTERONOMY 1:2; NUMBERS 13:17-33; PSALM 136

Introduction

For better or for worse, history often repeats itself. If we don't learn from past mistakes, we are doomed to repeat them. But if we learn from the past, we can walk into the future with hope and joy. We don't have to fall into the same pits and patterns as those who have gone before us.

Reading the history of Israel is an example of how the same sin-filled patterns can repeat themselves over and over again. The sin of grumbling was like a virus among the people. It kept spreading and it kept coming back again and again. Idolatry was the same. Add in the repetition of fear-driven faithlessness and you begin to see how the sins of God's people cycled through generation after generation. The only way things were going to change was if the people looked back over their history and learned from the past.

What was true for the nation of Israel thousands of years ago is just as true for us today. Wisdom calls us to learn from the past. Good examples should be identified and followed. Bad examples should be avoided. It is the wise person who looks back at the lessons God's people have already learned and takes these things to heart for life today.

Looking at Life

Pick *one* of the areas below and tell about a lesson you have learned from the past that has served you well in your life today.

1

- A lesson from your family
- A lesson from your nation's history
- A lesson from something a friend has faced
- A lesson from world history

Learning from the Word
Read: Exodus 3:7–10; 13:17–22; Deuteronomy 1:2

ARE WE THERE YET?

Anytime a family goes on vacation and they have little kids in the backseat, the kids will ask a question. They ask it often. They ask it irritatingly. They sometimes turn it into a chant or a song. The longer the trip is, the sooner they start with the question. The question, of course, is: "Are we there yet?"

Parents look forward to the day when kids mature and become patient, so that there's no more silly fighting over space violations, no more arguing over what radio station should get played, no more whining about where or when they're going to stop for lunch. They wait a long time for that day to come because, although most of us grow up, we never get much different.

As we grow older, we discover that our childlike chant "Are we there yet?" continues with some subtle adjustments. Now it sounds like this:

- "God, get me into this job and do it now."
- "Get me into this house, I need it soon."
- "Get me into this relationship, I can't wait."
- "Get me into this financial condition, I can't hold on any longer."
- "Are we there yet? Are we there yet? Are we there yet?"

What God knew for the people of Israel, he still knows for us today. Having a portfolio flowing with dollars or a job flowing with power doesn't matter nearly as much as having a character that flows with the fruit of the Spirit. God is still more concerned with who we are becoming than with how quickly we get to our desired destination.

The trip that took Israel forty years could have been made in a matter of weeks. What were some of the heart conditions in his people that God was trying to change during those forty years?

2

3

Describe a time that God took you on a longer path than you would have preferred. As you look back, what was God doing in your life during this time?

HOW'S YOUR MEMORY?

The Israelites have just been delivered from Pharaoh and his army. They have crossed the Red Sea, and God has given them miraculous redemption. The mighty hand of God has been revealed in power through plagues, a pillar of fire, and deliverance from the hand of the most powerful ruler on the face of the earth at that time. It would seem that this manifestation of God's presence and power would leave a lasting and indelible impression on the people of Israel. It would be natural to think that the impact of these events would stay with them forever. But notice how quickly they forget. In just three days they are discouraged, grumbling, and angry.

It takes only three days for the people to forget all God has done for them. God has delivered them from Egypt, performed the ten plagues, and drowned Pharaoh and his army in the sea. You would think their faith should be unshakable after all of this. But just three days later, God is at the wheel driving and the kids are in the backseat whining and complaining. They have forgotten. Their short memory is evidence of the fact that they have missed the profound spiritual reality that God is with them.

Read: Exodus 15:22–24; 16:6–12

4

Describe the attitude of God's people in these passages and explain how you think they could see so many miracles and still have these heart conditions.

5

Remembering what God has done in the past helps us live with confidence for our future. What are some practical actions we can take, memorials we can set up, or practices we can put in place to help us remember the great things God has done in our lives?

Read: Exodus 16:13–32

THE MANNA PRINCIPLE

Here is the manna principle: one day at a time. God will provide for you one day at a time. Trust God for this day right now. In the days of Moses, some people got anxious, others got greedy, and still others grew fearful. Some people thought they'd beat the system by gathering tomorrow's manna. God had something important to teach them—and us as well. It is the manna principle by which we are to live. God says, "I want you to live your life trusting me one day at a time—just this day. Learn to trust me for this day. If you start worrying about tomorrow, you are going to worry your whole life long."

We don't need to ask for guarantees about tomorrow. We don't need to ask for answers to questions we are not being asked yet. We don't need to ask for the ability to cross a bridge that we haven't yet reached. Each of us needs to learn to pray, "God, I'll trust you for this day, my daily bread, today. And when I wake up tomorrow morning, like manna, your mercies will be new once again."

6

As you look at this passage and reflect on the manna principle by which the people of Israel, who actually collected and ate the manna, lived, how would you respond to *one* of the following statements?

- I live with a lot of worry that I won't have enough saved when I finally retire.
- If I can save enough and invest enough, I know I will finally feel at peace and be confident about my future.

- I want to live with trust that God will provide manna for each day, so I am going to stop working, stop exerting any personal effort, and just trust God to meet all my needs.
- I know that if I am going to make ends meet, I have to work seven days a week. I can't afford to take a Sabbath day for rest and worship.

7 Tell about a time when God opened heaven and rained down his provision of manna for you in an amazing and wonderful way.

> All we want in Christ, we shall find in Christ. If we want little, we shall find little. If we want much, we shall find much; but if, in utter helplessness, we cast our all on Christ, he will be to us the whole treasury of God.
> **HENRY BENJAMIN WIPPLE**

8 Sometimes God provides the manna we need through other people. What can you do, as a small group, to be instruments of God's provision for someone in your church or community who needs to see God provide manna in their life?

A GRASSHOPPER COMPLEX

There is a poignant image in Numbers 13:32–33. The ten spies with the bad report say, "We can't attack those people; they are stronger than we are." And they also say, "The land we explored devours those living in it. All the people we saw there are of great size. . . . We seemed like grasshoppers in our own eyes, and we looked the same to them." Not only do the spies feel like grasshoppers with no strength. They let the poison of their fear spread through the people of Israel until the entire nation has a grasshopper complex.

Many of these people have never really recovered from the "slave mentality" they learned in their years of bondage in Egypt. As far back as they can remember, all they have ever been is somebody's slave. The tragedy is that this generation will never see themselves as anything but grasshoppers. They will not allow hope and joy to fill their hearts. They will not allow themselves to trust God for the great adventure he wants to lead them through.

Some people today live with a deep-seated grasshopper complex. If the truth were known, they would say, "I look in the mirror and all I see is a grasshopper. I'm not adequate. I'm not competent. I'm not strong enough." But the issue isn't whether we are adequate or competent or strong enough. The question is: Are we willing to trust God one day at a time?

Read: Numbers 13:17–33

The spies come back with good and bad news about the land they have surveyed. Make a list of what they say about the land and the people who live there.

9

The good news about the land and the people who lived there:

The bad news about the land and the people who lived there:

The spies all see the same land, the same inhabitants, and the same set of obstacles. How does Caleb's faith influence the way he sees the call to occupy the land?

10

What is one step of faith you know God wants you to take, but one you have not yet moved forward?

What "giants in the land" are you facing that make moving forward difficult for you?

Closing Reflection

Take a few minutes of silence for personal reflection . . .

Choose one of the four wilderness lessons that struck home for you and reflect on one of the questions below:

- What is one area of your life where you experience impatience? What might you learn about God and yourself as you need to learn patience here?

- What can you do to work at remembering the great things God has done in your past?

- How can you grow to trust God as the One who provides for you one day at a time? How can you embrace the manna principle and live with daily confidence in God's provision?

- When do you most often feel helpless and small, like a grasshopper? What needs to happen in your heart and life for you to grow more confident in this area of your life?

Take time to respond to this closing question:

Of the four wilderness lessons, which one seems to apply most to where you are in your life right now? How can your group members pray for you and encourage you to walk in the reality of this lesson?

Close your small group by praying together.

- Pray for yourself as you seek to apply the wilderness lesson God brought to your heart through this study.

- Pray for your group members as they seek to apply the lesson they have learned for their lives.

- Pray for all of your group members to learn to live with wise hearts that learn from the past in a way that brings joy to their future.

Old Testament Life Challenges

SETTING UP MEMORIALS

All through the Old Testament, God calls the people of Israel to remember what he has done for them. One of the practical reminders they used was setting up a pile of stones as a memorial so that they could see this visible sign and remember what God has done for them (Joshua 4:4–7). We, like the people of Israel, are prone to forget. We need to learn how to set up piles of stones that will remind us of the great things God has done for us.

Maybe we don't actually pile up rocks, but there are ways we can remember God's goodness in our past. Some people keep a list of answered prayers to remind them of God's power and faithfulness. Others make a point of retelling stories of what God has done in their past (Psalm 136). There are people who will capture a great moment of spiritual growth or learning with a photograph they display or in a poem or picture they have created. The key concern is not what we use as a reminder as much as that we remember God's goodness in our lives. Take time this week to pile up some stones somewhere in your life. Set up a memorial to remind you of something God has done for you.

A PRAYER FOR MANNA

Commit to lift up the manna prayer, written below, every day of the coming week. Let this prayer move you to a place of trust, confidence, and thankfulness!

> *God, give me manna for today, just this day. Give me enough wisdom. Give me enough patience. Give me enough courage. Give me enough love to handle this day. And as best I can, God, I'll trust that when I wake up in the morning, you'll be there with me and you'll help me face tomorrow. I'm not going to try to collect more from you than I need. I want to learn to trust you for this day. Amen.*

What Indiana Jones Was Looking For

SESSION 8: EXODUS 24-30

Introduction

Most of us dream about the kind of place we'd like to live someday. There are all kinds of magazines, TV shows, web sites, and books devoted to home building and improvement. Our homes take up a good amount of our time and finances. But even with all we put into them, most of us still have a list of changes we want to make and things we want to fix. For some of us, this list gets longer and longer as the years pass. If we look at our homes and our plans for improvement, we can learn a lot about what matters to us.

When the people of Israel lived in the wilderness, they discovered that God wanted to have a home among them. The tabernacle gave the people a visual picture of how God wanted to be in the very center of their lives. God had his people arrange their lives, physically and spiritually, around the tabernacle. When they set up camp, the tent of meeting was to be in the center. Then the priests and Levites camped around the tent. Finally, all the tribes of Israel camped surrounding the tabernacle. There were three tribes on the north, three on the south, three on the east, and three on the west. The door of each tent faced the tabernacle.

The entire community was built around the tabernacle. They all knew that this tent in the middle of their camp represented God's presence in their midst. When they moved to a new location, the pieces of the tabernacle were carried in the middle of the population. This was a way of physically picturing that they were to be a community centered on God. If we look closely at the tabernacle as a picture of God's house, we can learn a lot about what matters to him.

Looking at Life

1

By looking at your home, what do you think a visitor would say is central in your life?

Why would they say this is so important to you?

Learning from the Word
Read: Exodus 24:17–18; 25:8–9

GOD IS WITH US

The instructions for what God's dwelling place should look like begin in Exodus 25. Moses went up the mountain, stayed there forty days and forty nights, and came back with instructions for the tabernacle. During the time God's people were at Mount Sinai, they saw the presence of the Lord, and it was glorious. It was like a cloud on the mountain. You can be sure they would have loved to see that glory stay in such a powerful and visible way, but it did not.

God wanted his people to know he would be with them, even when the mountain was not consumed in fire, so he showed them a new way to experience his presence. In Exodus 25, God began to give instructions about the building of the tabernacle, his dwelling place. The tabernacle was a visible sign of the presence of God with his people. When the people of God saw the tabernacle, they could say, "God is with us!"

2

What are some of the ways (in this passage and other parts of the Old Testament) that God revealed his presence and showed his people he was with them?

3

What are some of the ways God reveals his presence today and shows us he is still with us?

> The best way to prepare for the coming of Christ is to never forget the presence of Christ.
>
> **WILLIAM BARCLAY**

Read: 1 Corinthians 6:19–20

4

Where is the new dwelling place of God's Spirit, and what has made this possible?

THE HOUSE OF GOD

The tabernacle was to be the dwelling place of God (Leviticus 26:11).
It is important to note that the tabernacle and its furnishings were built along the lines of a Near Eastern home. If you could have visited the home of a Near Eastern nomad at that time, you would have noticed that the structure of the average tent dwelling place was similar to the tabernacle. The objects placed in the tabernacle would also have been found in most homes in that day. They would have been made of more common materials, but the basic concept was the same.

The tabernacle had a large outer courtyard, which was about half the size of a football field. This outer courtyard was enclosed by a structure with wooden frames and brilliant curtains that could be torn down and transported. Much like a fenced-in yard in our day, these frames and curtains offered a kind of safe, quiet place for people to gather and meet with God. Inside the tabernacle was a whole assortment of objects, and each one had great spiritual significance.

At this time in your small group, you should take about five minutes for personal reading. Each small group member will choose from one of the five articles of furnishing from the tabernacle listed below and study a selected passage from the Bible as well as the brief reading about that article. If you have time, you also might want to draw attention to the additional notes in the back of this study (in the Leader's Notes) on the item you choose to study.

Choose one of the articles listed below for personal study.

Read: Exodus 27:1-8 for the bronze altar

As a person entered the courtyard of the tabernacle, the first object they would have noticed would be the altar. In the homes in those days there was generally some kind of grill or pit for cooking food. In the tabernacle the bronze altar for sacrifices was the equivalent of the grill in a home. It was about 7 -1/2 feet square and about 4 -1/2 feet high. There were horns on each side, and animals were tied to them before being offered as a sacrifice. It was on this altar that the many different sacrifices were placed. The people knew that this was the place where sin was paid for and restitution was made.

Read: Exodus 30:17-21 for the basin

The next thing someone would see as they entered the courtyard of the tabernacle was the basin. This was a large, bronze basin where the priests would cleanse themselves before and after washing the sacrifice. This would have been recognized as a common amenity in a ancient Near Eastern home. People entered homes quite dusty and dirty and needed to clean up. In many homes there was a bowl or basin of water near the entrance. In our hyperclean society we can't imagine what it would be like to be dirty most of the time. But in those days, when a person entered a dwelling, there was often a basin for cleansing. In the tabernacle, the parallel piece of furniture was the basin, which functioned as the place of cleansing.

Read: Exodus 25:31–40 for the lampstand

The lampstand stood in the outer chamber of the Holy Place. It was made of pure hammered gold. The priest's job was to keep it filled with olive oil so that the flame would never go out. It remained lit all through the night. Like a home at that time in history, there was always a light burning. Why? This was the one part of the tabernacle that could be seen from the outside. This ever-burning light was like a person who leaves a porch light on to send a message that somebody's home. Anybody in Israel could come to the courtyard, even at night, when they were alone or when they were worried, and there was a light on in God's house. The people of God knew that somebody was always home.

Read: Exodus 30:1–10 for the altar of incense

When you entered the Holy Place, you would see the altar of incense. In homes in the ancient Near East, people often burned incense to cover up the odor of people who did not bathe often, animals that lived in the house, and the smell of animals that had been slaughtered and cooked for family meals. The tabernacle had incense burning in the entry area of the Holy Place. This brought relief because the smell of slaughtered animals would have been intense throughout the entire tabernacle. In Revelation 5:8 we read about golden bowls full of incense. We are told that these are the prayers of the saints, a sweet thing to God. Incense is a picture of a sweet aroma ascending to God. As God's people, we need to learn that our prayers are sweet to God and that they ascend to his throne like fragrant incense.

Read: Exodus 25:23–30 for the bread of the Presence

In the entrance to the Holy Place was also the table of the Presence. It was built of wood and covered with gold. The serving utensils also were made of gold. The primary purpose of this table was to hold the bread of the Presence. Every week the priests were to bake twelve loaves for the twelve tribes of Israel. Twelve loaves of fresh bread were set out on a regular basis for everyone to see and smell. One of the reasons the bread was called "the bread of the Presence" was that it pointed to the warm, fresh, sweet presence of God. Literally the term meant "the bread of the face." This bread was always before the face of God. It thus reminded the people of Israel of God's face through his daily provision and fresh presence every day.

5

Which of the five articles did you choose to study and what have you learned *about the heart and character of God* from this piece of furniture in his house (tabernacle)?

6

Imagine you are walking into the tabernacle and you see the item of furniture you chose to study; what does this article teach you about *how you can prepare to worship God*?

7

What is one way you see the heart and ministry of Jesus reflected in the tabernacle?

ENTERING GOD'S PRESENCE

After passing through the Holy Place, seeing the light, and smelling the bread and incense, the priests come to a heavy curtain. It is a blue, purple, and scarlet veil, which separates the Holy Place from what is called "the Most Holy Place" (or "the Holy of Holies"). This curtain is the doorway to the room of greatest intimacy. This part of the tabernacle can be compared to a bedroom in a home. It is set aside for only the most intimate companion of God, the high priest.

In the Most Holy Place is a single piece of furniture—the ark of the covenant. This is a beautifully crafted box overlaid with pure gold. On top of the ark is the atonement cover (or mercy seat). Over the atonement cover are two golden cherubs, one at each end. Their wings spread out and overshadow the ark and the atonement cover. Today we tend to think of cherubs as cute, chubby little valentine figures. But that's not accurate, biblically speaking. These are mighty angelic beings of great power. Yet even the great forces in the universe are humbled before the awesome presence of God, so these beings are bowing down!

God actually tells his people that his presence will dwell above the atonement cover and between the two cherubim. It is as if God is saying, "I'll come and sit on a box in a tent, and you will know I'm always with you. I will guide you." What an amazing picture of God's willingness to be present with his people, right where they are.

Read: Exodus 25:10-22; Hebrews 9:1-5

In light of what you learn about God's presence among his people both in the Old and New Testaments, how would you respond to someone who makes the following statement?

> *I don't have a problem believing in a god or some kind of higher power, but I believe this god got things started in the universe and has left us to figure it out. If there is some kind of god or life force out there, it certainly has no interest in being involved with us in any personal way.*

9

Three items are placed in the ark as an everlasting reminder to the people of Israel. What are these articles, and why are they such important reminders of God's work in their past?

Read: Exodus 16:32–33; 32:15–16; Numbers 17:10

10

Choose one of the items kept in the ark of the covenant and tell what this object teaches you about how God wants to work in your life today.

How does this item gives you hope for your future?

Closing Reflection

Take a few minutes of silence for personal reflection . . .

It was the desire of God's heart to dwell in the center of his people as individuals and a community. Their community and lives were to be built around his presence (both spiritually and literally). Take a moment and reflect on where God is in your life today. Use the graph below to indicate where you believe God fits into your life:

Take time to respond to this closing question:

Where does God fit in your life today, and what can you do to make him more central?

Close your small group by praying together.

- Pray that each of your group members will have a growing awareness of God's presence in their lives.

- Ask God to teach all of you to live in a way that makes room for him at the center of your lives.

- Thank God for his amazing provision of daily bread for all your needs.

Old Testament Life Challenges

MY SACRIFICE

There are many ways we can offer ourselves as living sacrifices:

- We can offer up a sacrifice of thanksgiving and praise as we cry out, "Thank you, God."

- We can offer our hearts in confession as we say, "I want to confess my sin and my sorrow to you. Cleanse me and change my heart and life."

- We can offer up surrendered lives as we pray, "God, I'll obey you even if it's painful. I will stay on the altar and let you do what you will with my life."

The altar may not be sitting in the entrance area of the tabernacle. But it still exists, and we are called to lay down our lives on it every day!

Take time this week to pray about how you can offer your life as a living sacrifice (Romans 12:1). What areas do you need to surrender today?

CLEANSE ME, LORD
The presence of the tabernacle in the middle of the camp served as a visual reminder that God was with his people. When they saw the tabernacle, they realized God was with them—leading, guiding, and watching. This impacted the way they related to each other and to God.

Pick a day in the coming week and do a spiritual experiment. Imagine Jesus is walking at your side every step of the day. Find some way to remind yourself of your commitment to think in this way through the day. For example, put a sticky note on your briefcase, an alarm in your hand-held computer that goes off with a reminder every thirty minutes, an object in your purse that will remind you, or something else that will function as a reminder throughout the day. Throughout your day ask simple questions such as these:

- Would I do or say this if Jesus were here with me in the workplace?

- Would I behave this way if Jesus were present with me on my school campus?

- What if Jesus were right here with me behind these closed doors?

- How would Jesus feel about this decision?

- What if Jesus were with me every moment of every day?

Loving God's Law

SESSION 9: TEXTS FROM EXODUS, LEVITICUS, AND DEUTERONOMY

Introduction

The law was Israel's prized possession. In Deuteronomy 4:5–14 we see that the laws of God were to be followed in such a way that the world would look on in amazement. The people of God knew that following the law would make them wise and discerning. They also knew that the world would be watching and would witness the presence and power of God as his people walked in obedience to his laws.

Moses called the people to reflect deeply on this question: "What other nation is so great as to have such righteous decrees and laws as this body of laws I am setting before you today?" (Deuteronomy 4:8). Their military force, wealth, or position in the eyes of the world did not establish their greatness. Their prized possession was not the tabernacle, Solomon's temple, or even the Promised Land once they entered. The people of Israel identified the law of God as the one thing that set them apart among the nations. It was their most valued treasure.

The people of Israel did not see the law of God as some whip-cracking taskmaster that ruled over them. They loved the law of God. They saw how it was lifting them out of the chaotic darkness of sin and closer to the heart of God.

Looking at Life

1

Tell about a prized possession you had during *one* of the seasons of life listed below:

- Your childhood
- Your teenage years
- Your life as a young adult
- Your life right now

What made this possession so valuable to you?

Learning from the Word

EXTRAVAGANT GENEROSITY

Many people think that the biblical call to give a tithe (the first 10 percent) of our income back to God is a huge sacrifice. The idea of giving 10 percent to God's work can feel like extravagant generosity. But consider what a faithful Israelite would give each year by simply following the teachings in God's law.

The tithe: 10 percent. All the way back in the Old Testament it was a fairly common practice for the people to give the first 10 percent of their income (harvest) to God. This expectation was clear then, and it is still in effect today.

The Sabbath year: 14 percent. For a faithful Israelite the giving didn't stop with a tithe. Out of concern for the earth, God says, "Every seventh year, people are not to plant anything. No sowing, no reaping, let the land rest." In an agricultural economy this Sabbath rest for the land would have cost the people a full year of income every seven years.

Jubilee year: 2 percent. The Old Testament also teaches that every forty-nine years God declared a year of Jubilee. Like the Sabbath year, it was a time when the earth rested and there was no planting or harvesting. During this time debts were forgiven and people were set free from bondage.

Gleaning laws: 4–5 percent. God called the people to leave some produce behind in the fields when they harvested. His people were to be a little sloppy when they farmed. These laws moved them to show tender compassion on the poor and needy. They were to leave something in the fields and on the trees so the poor could come through and get a little harvest to help meet their need. It's hard to estimate what percentage of income the Israelites would lose from doing this, but a safe guess would be 4–5 percent.

Extravagant generosity: 30 percent or more! The total amount a person who faithfully observed the law would have given was an average of 30 percent of their income to God and to those in need.

Read: Deuteronomy 15:1–11; 24:19–22; Leviticus 27:30; 25:2–5; 25:8–12

2 In light of these passages, what do you learn about how God views our finances?

3 How might our lives and society be different if we still followed these various forms of generous giving?

> **M**an should not consider his outward possessions as his own, but as common to all, so as to share them without hesitation when others are in need.
>
> **THOMAS AQUINAS (THIRTEENTH CENTURY)**

4 What is one step you could take to increase your generosity toward people?

What is one step you could take to become more generous toward God?

THREE GREAT TIMES OF CELEBRATION

Passover: In Deuteronomy 16:1–8 we read about God's call for his people to remember and celebrate their independence from Egypt. The Passover marked their deliverance from bondage and the time they became free as a nation. The Fourth of July is our closet equivalent to this ancient celebration. Passover was when the people of God became independent from Egypt. God called them to have a celebration for a whole week once a year. Their job was to eat, rejoice, remember, be thankful, and to celebrate what God had done for them. Only a God of joy would command his people to have a week-long festival every year!

The Feast of Weeks: The second great festival of Israel, found in Deuteronomy 16:9–12, is called the Feast of Weeks. This came during the latter part of the growing season when they had just begun to take in the first crops. In our calendar year the holiday that marks the end of summer, when we honor the work that has been done, is Labor Day. This feast was a time to celebrate all the work that had been done and God's provision through the harvest.

The Feast of Tabernacles or Booths: The third great feast is described in Deuteronomy 16:13–17. It's called the Feast of Tabernacles (or Booths). The idea was that people would actually live in tents to remember the time they lived in portable dwellings in the wilderness. This celebration came after the entire harvest had been brought in. In our calendar the time we remember our earliest settlers thanking God for the harvest is Thanksgiving Day. This is the best modern-day equivalent to remind us of the spirit of the Feast of Booths.

Read: Deuteronomy 16:1–17

When some people read the Old Testament, they get the idea that God is a sober and angry taskmaster who never wants his children to have any fun. How do these three festivals challenge this view of God?

5

6

In light of Deuteronomy 16, respond to *one* of the statements below:

- A pastor is preaching and says, "Followers of Christ should be the most joy-filled people in the entire world!"

- A Christian says, "I don't have time to celebrate, rejoice, or have little festivals; I am too busy serving God!"

- An unbeliever says, "I would never want to become a Christian; Christians never have any fun!"

7

What is one way you have learned to enjoy God's goodness?

What is one thing you could do to help you grow in your ability to rejoice and celebrate?

EAGLES, ROBINS, AND PIGEONS

Back in the early years of grade school there were often three reading groups. The teacher pretended that these groups were the same, but everyone knew this was not the case. You could tell which group was on the top and which was on the bottom by their names. For instance, you might have the "eagles" as one group—of course, they were the best readers. Then there might be the "robins"—these students could read fairly well, but they still needed some work. Finally, there would be the "pigeons"—these kids knew they would not be soaring with the eagles.

As we look back at the people of Israel at this time in their history, they were in the pigeon group. Spiritually speaking, they were not eagles or even robins. They were the pigeons. That is why it took them forty years to take an eleven-day walk. This is not the advance-placement class. They were barely making passing grades.

Read: Exodus 21:22–24; Matthew 5:38–42

What is the spirit and feeling of Exodus 21:23–25 when it comes to the topic of retribution, and what is the spirit and feeling of Matthew 5:38–42 on the same topic?

8

How can both of these passages be inspired by the same God?

STARTING WHERE WE ARE

God has to start where people are. We must remember that when Exodus was first written, there were no prior Scriptures, no written law of God. Although history teaches us that there were some written moral codes in existence by this time (such as the *Code of Hammurabi*), it is clear that in general the world was in a moral dark age. It was in relational, spiritual, and moral chaos. There were all kinds of common practices that would be shocking today. Child sacrifice was practiced and was even part of some religious rituals in pagan worship. Radical revenge and retribution was acceptable. If someone was wronged, his community often took revenge on a whole family rather than just the person who offended him. In some cases, they took vengeance on a whole city. Cult prostitution existed all over this part of the ancient world, and the people of Israel saw this as a normative practice.

As God began to call a community of people to follow him, he started where they were. In a society of immorality, he began to introduce steps so they could understand. God was dealing with pigeons, so he did not give instructions that only eagles could follow. In a similar way, God meets each of us where we are and begins to lead us to where he wants us to be.

9

God spoke through Moses and gave basic first steps in the area of revenge. Later, Jesus gave more advanced instructions when people were ready to hear the deeper truth. How has God met you where you are in your spiritual growth and then taken you to a deeper level months or even years later?

10

What is one area in which you have felt God calling you to a deeper level of growth and devotion?

How can your small-group members support and pray for you as you take steps forward in this area of your life?

Closing Reflection

Take a few minutes of silence for personal reflection . . .

Are you growing in your love for God's law? Do you feel your "passion for the Bible" getting deeper as the years pass? What disciplines do you need to put in place in your life so that you have a consistent flow of biblical truth into your heart and life?

Take time to respond to this closing question:

What steps are you going to take to grow in your knowledge and love of God's law (his Word)?

Close your small group by praying together:

- Ask the Holy Spirit to give you and your small-group members a spirit of joy and celebration.

- Pray for a deeper love for God's Word.

- Pray for discipline to study the Bible in a consistent and disciplined manner.

- Invite the Holy Spirit to move you forward in your spiritual journey. Let him know that you want to soar like an eagle rather than flutter like a pigeon.

Old Testament Life Challenges

PAUSE FOR REFLECTION: WHAT DO I LOVE?

The people of God showed their love for his law by spending vast amounts of time studying it, speaking of it often, committing it to memory, and letting it shape their lives. Take time in the next week to reflect on these questions:

- Where do I invest my time?

- What do I talk about most?

- What fills my mind the majority of the time?

- What shapes my life and actions?

- What can I do to grow in my love for God's Word?

- When and where do I experience a desire to know God's Word more?

LEAVE SOMETHING IN THE BAG

There are many ways we can apply what we learn from the laws of generosity in Leviticus and Deuteronomy. Most churches or communities have some kind of occasional food drive or a food pantry for those who are in a time of need. One simple discipline is to begin practicing a modern application of the ancient gleaning laws. This might mean committing to buy one or two additional items to give away each time you go to the store. When you get home, put these in a separate bag and set this aside. Once the bag is full, give it away.

LIFE APPLICATION: FEAST AND CELEBRATION DAYS

Take time to talk with your group about establishing an occasional feast and celebration day or evening. Plan to gather with the intention of eating foods you love, listening to music you enjoy, or doing things that are fun for you. You might even want to rotate who will lead the time so that you all get a sample of what brings joy and a spirit of celebration among your small-group members.

LEADER'S NOTES

C⊙ПTEПTS

THE HEART
of a Leader

As you prepare to lead this small-group session, take time to read Psalm 139:1–16. Reflect on how God feels about you. Celebrate that you are his child, "fearfully and wonderfully made." Ask the Holy Spirit to give you eyes to see yourself as his child and others as God's beloved children. Prepare to lead your small group with a heart that is in wonder and awe of how much God loves you and each person in your group.

THE PRAYER
of a Leader

Take time to pray for each of your small-group members by name as you prepare for your first study in this Old Testament Challenge series. Pray that you will be used by God and that each member of your small group will come to know God in more intimate and life-changing ways.

Group Members   **My Prayer**

_____   _____

_____   _____

_____   _____

_____   _____

_____   _____

_____   _____

_____   _____

LEADER'S NOTES

Question 1

Take time as a small group to reflect on the surprising and awesome power of our words. This lesson will help your group see how powerful the opening words of Genesis really are. Because our culture has been so influenced by the Old Testament, we can miss how radical these words and concepts were to the mind of a person who lived in Moses' day.

Note also the power of words in these opening chapters of the Bible as God speaks and all things come into existence. Words have power.

Question 2

Take time to look at how the worldview in the opening chapters of Genesis rivaled the conventional wisdom of the day. These words challenged the idea that there were many gods, even though these gods lacked real power and manifested immoral character. Rather, there was one supreme God filled with love, creativity, and interest in his people. This chapter also paints a whole new picture of the value of human beings as a group and each individual person. When that writer picked his stylus from the leather scroll and wrote the opening words of Genesis under the inspiration of God's Holy Spirit, the world was forever changed. The book of Genesis has changed the history of this world more than any other document, volume, or letter ever written.

The Bible is the best-selling book in the history of the world, and its teachings continue to change our views of God, the world, and the people around us. The greatest minds in the human race have devoted themselves to studying this book. Many people have moved to foreign countries and studied foreign cultures and languages so the Bible could be translated and so that people all over the world could read it. People have sacrificed their lives and have gone to prison for this book. It is God's great gift to us!

Question 3

Take time to reflect on the presence of the Trinity from the very beginning of creation. Make note of the community that existed even in the creation of the world:

In verse 1 we see the **Father** creating. In James 1:17 this Creator is called "the Father of the heavenly lights," from whom comes "every good and perfect gift."

In verse 2 the **Spirit** of God is hovering over the waters. Similar language is used to describe the Spirit of God hovering over Jesus at his baptism.

In verse 3 God creates by speaking his word. In the beginning of the gospel of John we learn that "the Word," through which all things are created, is none other than Jesus Christ, the **Son of God** (John 1:1; 14).

Out of this community, this Trinitarian joy and delight, God creates. He does not do this because he is bored or lonely. God does not create us so that he will have little servants to do the chores he does not want to do. Rather, out of the magnificent richness of the eternal community experienced by the Trinity, God decides to broaden the circle. He longs to invite us to live in his love. This invitation is not for us to become little gods; it is for us to bask in the glorious fellowship of the Trinity.

Questions 4–6

As human beings, we live with the risk of forgetting who we are. We live between two radically different extremes. On the one end, we can become prideful and believe we deserve a place equal to God. Sadly, this happened early in human history, and it still happens today. On the other end of the continuum is an attitude that degrades human beings and treats them as some coincidental result of a random big bang and cosmic accident.

Between these poles lies the truth. We are God's creation. Human beings are the apex, the pinnacle of God's creative work. Yet, we are not God; we are his children. We are valuable because of who made us, and we are significant because of how he made us—in his image! Yet we must never forget that he is the Creator and we are his creation.

We need to notice when we read of the creation of human beings that we are finite, limited, and fragile. We are not gods. We are made of dust. It is important to note that everything else in Genesis 1–2 was spoken into existence. We receive a great message of perspective a chapter later in Genesis 3:19: We came from dust and we will return to dust.

Questions 8–10

We get confused. All of us do, sometimes. We forget that only the Creator is to be worshiped, never the creation. In the time Genesis was written, people worshiped the sun, moon, stars, and even handmade stone idols. Fortunately we have moved well beyond that kind of adoration of material things—or have we?

Many people have become entangled in new forms of idolatry. Let some of these words float through your mind for a moment: Lexus, Beemer, my portfolio, or the summer cottage. Material things still cry out for our worship, and we need to get a proper perspective on the stuff of this world. We need to remember who made it all, who sustains it all, and who truly deserves our worship and adoration.

LEADER'S NOTES

THE HEART
of a Leader

This is a study that will invite the Holy Spirit to come and lay our hearts open before the Father. We will look into the mirror to see ourselves as God sees us. Here is the difficult truth: The reflection we see is not always attractive!

As a small-group leader, take time to search your own heart and ask God to show you if there is hidden sin within you. Take time to read and reflect on Psalm 51 (the prayer of confession David lifted to God after a time of serious sin and brokenness). Ask God to prepare your heart to lead your small group. Also, ask the Spirit to prepare your heart to receive what God wants to teach you.

THE PRAYER
of a Leader

Through history, God's people have used the book of Psalms as a prayer book. Take time in the days leading up to your small-group study to reflect deeply on Psalm 51. Spend time praying the first two verses of this psalm as you prepare to lead your small group when they gather.

Also, take time to memorize James 4:7 and meditate on it during the week prior to this study. Make this brief but powerful verse of Scripture part of your prayer life for the week leading up to this study.

As you prepare for your small group, take time to pray for each of your small-group members by name. Pray that their hearts will be soft and ready to receive a challenge to turn from sin and resist temptation.

Group Members   **My Prayer**

_____   _____

_____   _____

                          _____

_____   _____

                          _____

_____   _____

                          _____

Questions 1–2

God's plan is for us to experience deep and intimate community with him and with each other. This was his intention from the beginning. So, when we feel the warmth and security of a loving community, we discover a core part of God's plan for us. The opposite is true as well. When we feel ostracized and excluded, there is a depth of pain because we are living outside God's intended plan. Take time as a small group to talk about how it feels to be in community and how we feel when community is broken.

Questions 3–4

Adam and Eve had everything they needed. God provided a paradise beyond what any of us could imagine. They had access to all the fruit of the garden—with one explicit exception.

What follows is tragic. Rather than celebrating what they had, they fixated on what they did not have. Rather than enjoying what was in-bounds, they wanted what was out-of-bounds. What follows is an account of the temptation they faced and how they fell, and the staggering consequences of this rebellion. Along with the unveiling of the tempting tactics of the devil, we see the relentless love of God for his children.

The enemy comes into the picture early in human history. He is not called Satan in this story, but the Christian church came to identify the serpent with the evil one. What follows is a brilliant exposition of how temptation works. This was true at the beginning of time, and it is just as true today!

As a group, be sure you take time to read the text box with the title, "A Look at the Serpent's Tactics." Also, look closely at Genesis 3. The tactics of the enemy have not changed much over the history of humanity. He is still the father of lies. He still seeks to twist our perception of God. As you look at this passage, take time to really identify how the enemy uses the same kinds of deception in our lives today.

Questions 5–6

Now things get a little personal. It is one thing to talk about sin in vague generalities. It is a whole different thing to confess your places of vulnerability. Be prepared as a leader to share your heart with your small group. Take time to reflect on the tactics the enemy uses to trip you up. Pray for your group members to have soft and humble hearts that are willing to take the counsel of James, and "confess your sins to each other and pray for each other" (James 5:16).

LEADER'S NOTES

Temptation is the tempter looking through the keyhole into the room where you are living. Sin is drawing back the bolt and making it possible for him to enter.

J. WILBUR CHAPMAN

Question 7

Be sure to read the text box titled "The Consequences of Sin." As you read this and the passage from Genesis, you will see dramatic changes that came once sin entered into the human experience.

Question 8

The old theological language for the human condition after sin entered is *depravity*. This is the birth of shame and guilt. People in our day often speak about the basic goodness of human beings. As Christians, we believe it is very good that God made human beings. We matter to him immensely, and we were made in God's image. It is also true that human beings often do good things. But followers of Christ understand that because of the Fall, human beings are not simply neutral, moral agents, who can always choose to do good if we just try hard enough.

Here is the truth: Just as glass is predisposed to shatter and nitroglycerin is predisposed to explode, we are predisposed to do wrong when the conditions are right. Theologically, that human predisposition is called depravity. In the days of the Reformation, great Christian thinkers even talked about *total depravity*. The main idea of this expression is that depravity affects all of us—not just our behavior but also our thoughts and our feelings. God's Word is clear that we cannot fix this problem on our own. We need God's help.

The most brilliant discussion of the topic of depravity that I know is in Dallas Willard's book *The Spirit of the Disciplines* (chapter 11). He doesn't use the word "depravity," but he addresses this issue. Here is my paraphrase of what Dallas writes:

> *Depravity is a spiritual condition that involves our readiness to harm others or at least let harm come to them if that will help us reach our goals of security, ego-gratification, of the satisfaction of our deep desires. Depravity is this: We would like to do what's right, but we're prepared to do what's wrong if we feel it's necessary for our survival or well-being.*

Questions 9-10

Genesis 3 holds both bad news and good news. The bad news is the reality and cost of sin. The good news is that God is already seeking to heal the broken bonds of community. When we struggle with sin, we run from God in many ways. For some people, their shame drives them away from Christian community. They stop coming to church, they drop out of their small group, and they avoid Christian friends. For others, the shift is more internal. They stop praying, they no longer hunger for God's Word, and their heart grows cold toward God. In some cases, the shame can drive a follower of Christ to dive deeper and deeper into sin.

This is why confession is so critical. When we confess and seek God's face again, we discover that we are still loved and that God longs to take away our shame. We need to remember that the same God who is pure and holy also loves us and started his work of restoration the moment human beings fell and entered into sin.

Genesis 3 is not all bad news. Tucked right in this section about sin, depravity, and the Fall are two hope-filled notes of grace. First, God tells the serpent (verse 15) that there will be enmity between the him and the woman (including her offspring); the serpent will strike at his heel, but the woman's offspring will crush the serpent's head. This passage is talking about Jesus Christ. Right after sin enters in, God is already giving a promise of salvation. Jesus will crush the enemy and destroy the power of sin (see Romans 16:20). This is the first prophetic mention of the coming of the Messiah in all of Scripture. It comes in response to the first sin.

Second, another grace note is seen when God makes garments of skin for Adam and Eve. At this point Adam and Eve are running around in stitched fig leaves, and they look severely fashion-challenged. So God becomes a tailor and clothes them so they can come into his presence without being overwhelmed by shame. What a picture of God's grace and love.

But if we look closely, we see there is even more going on here. Because the coverings God gave them are made of skin, a sacrifice has been made. For the first time in history, innocent blood has been shed so that human shame might be covered and fellowship with God restored. God is setting the stage for the Passover and, later, the death of Jesus as the sacrifice for our sins. What a powerful reminder of God's grace in these opening pages of the Bible.

LEADER'S NOTES

It's Time to DTR (Define the Relationship)

THE HEART
of a Leader

The God of Abraham is the same God we worship today. He still speaks, prompts, and leads his children. He still wants to have profound moments when he can do a DTR with each one of us. As you prepare your heart to lead your small group, invite God to do a DTR on you. Ask the Holy Spirit to search you and open your eyes to see areas you hunger for deeper places of faith and love.

Take time to read Psalm 139:23–24 and Psalm 103:1–5. Then wait in silence and invite the Spirit to challenge, convict, encourage, bless, or do whatever he wants to do in your heart. As you prepare to lead your small group, be sure you give God space to lead your relationship with him in new directions.

THE PRAYER
of a Leader

Take time to pray for each of your small-group members, including youself. Ask for the Holy Spirit to begin softening hearts and opening ears. Pray for relationships to be defined in new and fresh ways.

Question 1

We have all had many DTR moments in our lives. Some of these are humorous and light. When we look back, we can laugh and actually thank God for moving this relationship in a whole new direction. Some group members might have stories to tell that have happy endings.

At the same time, many of us have faced DTR moments that are still associated with deep pain. Some remember a broken engagement, a parent who walked away from the family, or a business relationship that exploded. These stories can be pain-filled and serious.

As a small-group leader, invite people to communicate on whatever level they feel fits their life experience. The key is seeing, in our lives and the lives of others, that we have all faced DTR moments in human relationships. This reality will help group members begin to identify how this same life experience can carry over into our relationship with God.

Questions 2–4

God has a single command for Abraham: Leave! Leave your country, your people, your tribe, and your father's household—everything safe and familiar. Implied in this is also the call to leave his old gods. Abraham does not know this God who is calling him to this radical step of faith. Listen to part of Joshua's speech to the Israelites as told in Joshua 24:2: "Long ago your forefathers, including Terah the father of Abraham and Nahor, lived beyond the River and worshiped other gods." Yet here is Abraham faced with an epic DTR moment. Will he stay, or will he leave and follow this God who is calling him?

There's an Old Testament principle here. It might be called the "principle of separation." God says, "Be separate from other gods—old values, old priorities—and be separate for the one true God." This principle was in effect for Abraham, and it is still in effect today for us.

We must understand the choice that Abraham is facing. Abraham is not some uncouth nomad with nothing to lose. He is a prosperous merchant. In verse 5 we read that he has accumulated many possessions, enough to have a whole retinue of servants and slaves. He lives in an urban setting in civilized Mesopotamia.

Haran, where Abraham's family came from, was located far in the northwest part of Mesopotamia. It is listed in Ezekiel 27:23 as one of the great commercial centers of the ancient world. It was on the Euphrates River. In that metropolitan center Abraham was known, respected, and secure. That was a place of safety and familiarity.

Yet, Abraham is told to leave for a wilderness where he has no lands, no networks, no connections, and no prospects. This move, humanly speaking, is financial, vocational, and maybe literal suicide. What kind of person follows a call like that? Only a person who has faith. Only a person who trusts without seeing can follow the way Abraham follows God!

WORD STUDY: ABRAHAM WENT

The whole story of Abraham (in a sense, the whole story of the Old Testament) hinges on a single phrase in Genesis 12:4. In Hebrew it's two words—*wayyelek ʾabram*. It means "Abraham went" or "Abraham left." As we read these two words, it is important to remember that Abraham is seventy-five years old. Just think about it: Abraham is seventy-five years old, and he chooses to bet everything on God. He goes, he leaves, he takes a step of faith!

LEADER'S NOTES

Questions 5-6

Abraham and Sarah faced the same pain many couples face today. They longed to have a child, but Sarah was not able to conceive. They longed to raise a child of their own. They dreamed of their family line going on beyond their generation. Yet year after year, decade after decade, Sarah did not conceive.

In all of this, Abraham and Sarah still sought to follow God and grew to love him more and more. Yet Abraham did something consistent with Old Testament spirituality, but something that is rare today. Abraham poured out his heart, his pain, his sorrow before God. He told God how he felt.

If you read the book of Psalms, you will quickly learn how common this practice of pouring out pain and sorrow was in the spiritual lives of God's people. Over one-third of the psalms are laments, where the person praying expresses honest and deep pain to God. Abraham cried out to God, and his heavenly Father hears and answers!

Question 7

When we understand the cost of broken covenants in the Old Testament, we discover the power of Jesus' words when he says, "This cup is the new covenant *in my blood*." The old covenant had been broken by sinful human beings. The covenant was violated. Somebody had to pay. Jesus said, "I'll pay. I'll suffer. I will pay the price that my children deserve, and then I will cut a new, unforgettable, and unshakable covenant with my blood. I will be cut. I will cut a covenant with my body." When we have this picture in our minds, coming to the communion table takes on a whole new level of significance. We realize that the punishment we deserve was paid for by Jesus.

Questions 8-10

Among the many lessons we can learn from the story of Abraham and Isaac is that God does not affirm human sacrifice. In those days, many of the people in that region did offer their children as sacrifices. The Ammonites were known for their devotion to a false god they called Molech. They often sacrificed children to him. But God warned the people of Israel: "Do not give any of your children to be sacrificed to Molech, for you must not profane the name of your God. I am the LORD" (Leviticus 18:21). Unlike the false gods that were worshiped in that region, the God of Abraham would not tolerate human or infant sacrifice. Life is too sacred!

Along with this lesson, Abraham learned about trust on a level most of us cannot begin to comprehend. But as we study the life of Abraham, we discover that God can take us to deeper places of faith and trust. Like Abraham, we don't always understand why we face hard decisions and painful choices. But when we follow God's leading, we always find ourselves closer to God and more mature as his followers.

LEADER'S NOTES

THE HEART
of a Leader

As you prepare to bring this message, take time for personal reflection. Identify times you have felt very alone. How did you respond to these feelings? How did you experience the presence of God during these times of your life? It will be important for you to hold these experiences in your heart as you teach. As you speak about God's presence, even in the hardest of times and the strangest of places, be aware of God's presence with you right now as well.

THE PRAYER
of a Leader

In this small-group session we will discover that God is with us, no matter what. Through the book of Genesis we see God reminding his people of his presence and care for them. In the moments they feel most alone, abandoned, and fearful, they hear God's persistent reminder that he is with them.

Begin praying that your small-group members will have rich encounters with God as a result of this study. Take time to look back over your own life. How have you experienced God being with you? As you prepare to lead, let your heart be filled with rich memories of God's revealing his presence in times of joy and sorrow. Take time to lift up prayers of deep thankfulness for God's faithfulness to be with you from the first days of your life.

Questions 1-2

Children have heroes that range from cartoon characters to family members to athletes. As we become adults, we also have heroes. We can see successful business people, great characters from history, movie and TV stars, characters from the Bible, or sports figures as heroes. There is nothing wrong with looking up to people who have accomplished great things, but we need to remember that they are still just people.

All through the Bible, God is clearly held up as *the* hero. It is God who creates, God who redeems, God who provides, and God who leads his people. As we study the Old Testament, we have a powerful opportunity to celebrate God as the hero of history—and the hero of our lives!

Questions 3–5

Isaac discovers God is with him in a unique way. It comes through the provision of a wife—through an amazing series of circumstances. Abraham is growing old, and he has experienced great blessing and provision from the hand of God. His son Isaac is now ready to marry, but Abraham is concerned about who his son's wife will be. So, he calls his chief servant in for an important meeting. We know Abraham's chief servant is Eliezer, so we can be fairly confident that he is the one who will carry out Abraham's plan. When Eliezer enters the room, Abraham asks him to place his hand under his thigh and swear by the Lord that he will do what Abraham is about to request.

In our day and age, we tend to seal an agreement with a handshake! This works well for most people. But in Abraham's day the tradition was different; placing a hand under a person's thigh was just part of the oath. It was as natural as shaking hands in our day, and it expressed a complete trust. In this oath, Eliezer promises that he will not get a wife for Isaac from the daughters of the Canaanites. Rather, he will find a wife for Isaac among Abraham's own people.

Question 6

All through the book of Genesis we see examples of parents playing favorites. Here is a key observation: It never works out well. There is never a sense that these actions and attitudes of favoritism bring life and health. They never lead to the edification of the children or the parents. Favoritism brings conflict, tension, and brokenness in each family.

What a sobering reminder to all those gathered who are parents or hope to be parents. It is also a good warning to grandparents and other family members, such as aunts and uncles. Beware of the danger of favoritism. God's Word teaches some good lessons about avoiding favoritism. Many of us have experienced the sting of growing up in a home where they were not "the favorite." God longs that this same dysfunction is not passed on to the next generation.

LEADER'S NOTES

WORD STUDY: ISRAEL

For much of his life his name is Jacob, the deceiver, and he lives out the meaning of his name. In Genesis 32, God gives him a new name, *Israel*. This new name points to his future. It means "he who struggles with God."

Questions 7–8

After wrestling with God and receiving a new name, Israel is a different person. Before all this happened, he devised a strategy to send groups with gifts ahead of him to meet Esau first and attempt to appease him. He also planned to have the rest of his family act as a buffer before he actually met his brother. Remember: The last time these two brothers were together, Esau wanted Jacob dead!

Before, Jacob fled in fear, but now he is Israel. He gathers his family and all he has and walks toward his brother. We read these words, "He himself went on ahead." He's the fighter. He's going first. He's leading the way. He'll take the risk. He's a new man.

As we read the story, we might expect Esau to come with anger and vengeance. We do read that he arrives to meet Jacob with four hundred men! This could have felt very threatening. But we read some of the most touching words in the Bible: "Esau ran to meet Jacob and embraced him; he threw his arms around his neck and kissed him. And they wept." It is a bit surprising, perhaps, to note that Esau's response is very much like the response of the father in the parable of the prodigal son in Luke 15:20. Esau models a heart of grace, love, and forgiveness. His heart is like the heart of God toward his wayward children. The long, slow, redemptive work of God bears fruit, and the dream of community wins a little bit. Finally, in this sad story, two brothers are reconciled.

One of the great statements in the Bible is found in Genesis 33:10. This is definitely a verse worth underlining in your Bible. Jacob says to Esau: "If I have found favor in your eyes, accept this gift from me. For to see your face is like seeing the face of God."

Now, "to see the face" in the Semitic language meant to know someone, to grasp their character. If someone's back is turned toward you, you can't see his or her character. But when they turn so you can see their face, you get to know their heart. You know what's going on inside of them.

Israel is stumbling slowly toward knowing more and more about God. As he grows to know God, it changes the way he sees people. He says, in effect, to his brother, Esau, "When you offer mercy, when you desire to reconcile, it reminds me of God. You remind me of God." The image of God begins to be a little more visible in human beings. It's just a beautiful statement: "For to see your face is like seeing the face of God."

Questions 9–10

Genesis 50:20 is a summary of Joseph's life. In a sense, it is a statement about the theology of Genesis. This short verse hits on a key Old Testament theme that helps us understand that God is at work and is with us even when we don't know it. Joseph's brothers feel certain that Joseph has wanted to kill them but has only held off because Jacob, his father, was still living. But now Jacob has died. At this point Joseph's brothers experience terror, throw themselves before him, and tell him, "We are your slaves." They're sure he's now ready to exact revenge on them.

Joseph replies, "Don't be afraid. I'm not angry with you. I'm not going to pronounce judgment on any of you." As they tremble in fear, knowing he can speak one word and have them executed for what they did to him so many years before, Joseph speaks these words, "You intended to harm me, but God intended it for good to accomplish what is now being done, the saving of many lives." Joseph realizes that God has been with him every step of the way and has had the entire history of his life planned out!

LEADER'S NOTES

THE HEART
of a Leader

God's delivering power and plans did not stop at the Passover lamb. They also did not stop at the cross and the empty tomb. The same God who worked miracles in Egypt and parted the Red Sea is ready to move in your life today. The same Jesus who rose from the grave on the first Easter is alive and ready to lead his people.

As you prepare for this small-group study, take time to evaluate your life habits, attitudes, and motives. Where do you feel stuck? What is one area of your life where you need God's deliverance? Ask God to reveal his delivering power in your life as you prepare to lead your small group.

THE PRAYER
of a Leader

We all need the deliverance that only God can offer. The starting point is when we come to a place where we realize our sin holds us captive and only God can save us through the shed blood of Jesus, the new Passover Lamb. As you prepare for this study, take time to thank God for sending his only Son as your deliverer. Also, pray for open eyes to see secret areas of sin in your life from which God wants to set you free. As you pray for your life, spend time praying for each of your group members. Ask the Holy Spirit to begin preparing their hearts to receive a powerful message of deliverance and freedom!

Questions 3–5

As we begin Exodus, the Israelites seem to be in an impossible situation. They are strangers in a strange land. They are oppressed. They are power-less. Humanly speaking, there is no way out. Yet God calls them to cling to him, even if their eyes see no hope of relief. In the same way, we need to hold fast to our God when the waters rise around us. No matter how bad the storm and no matter how great the enemy, our hope is in God.

God promised Abraham that his descendants would be like the sand of the seashore and the stars of the heavens. But as the book of Exodus opens, this great promise seems to be in jeopardy. Abraham, Isaac, Jacob, and Joseph are dead. Their descendants are slaves in a foreign land. The idea of a great nation of people populating the Promised Land must have seemed like a distant dream. To the human eye, it seemed as if hope was gone.

At the beginning of Exodus we hear a phrase that has become a refrain throughout the Pentateuch. We see a theme that is close to the heart of God. It is captured in these words: "Now Joseph and all his brothers and all that generation died, but the Israelites were fruitful and multiplied greatly and became exceedingly numerous, so that the land was filled with them."

You might remember the very first command God gave the human race. In Genesis 1:28 God said, "Be fruitful and increase in number." After the Flood God said to Noah and his family, "Be fruitful and increase in number." God came to Abraham and made a promise: "I will make you fruitful and give you many descendants." Abraham actually laughed because he did not think it was likely that he would be fruitful. But he and Sarah did have a son, and his descendants end up in Egypt. While they were in this furnace of oppression, they were fruitful and they multiplied greatly.

Who is at work here? It is God. The Israelites may not recognize it, but we can see it as we read the Bible and look back on what happened. It is no accident that the Israelites are proliferating like this. In the covenant, God promised Abraham that he would have more descendants than stars in the sky. This promise is coming true, even if the people of Israel do not recognize it.

Questions 6-7

Shiphrah and Puah are remarkable women. It is important that we remember their names. These two women defy a pharaoh and risk their lives in an act of heroism. They will not kill the boys. When the Pharaoh calls them in and asks them, "Why do you do this? Why do you let the boys live?" the women do not say to him, "It's because we fear God." Rather, they say, "Well, these Hebrew women are vigorous, and their babies pop out before we can get there."

This passage is not an affirmation of lying. If people ask whether this passage affirms lying, the short answer might be, "If you are ever coerced into committing mass murder by a genocidal maniac and the only way you can get out of this horrendous act is to deceive the genocidal maniac with a lie, I think God will understand." We don't want people to use this passage to justify the kind of self-serving deceit that most of us engage in that breaks community and destroys trust. This is not what God is trying to teach us in this passage.

It is interesting to note that the author of Exodus never mentions the pharaoh's name. The text never says which pharaoh Moses faces. In the hierarchy of Egypt, the pharaoh is at the top of the organizational chart while the midwives are at the very bottom. Midwives are the servants to the slaves. They don't count. But in God's organizational chart, the midwives are heroes. They risk their lives to accomplish his purposes.

When we read about them and see how God mentions them by name, it is as if God is saying, "These two women, who are nobodies in the eyes of the world, are the ones who go in my book." The first will be last. The humble will be exalted. This is the way God works.

Question 8

Like Moses, we can all make excuses for why we don't think God should use us for his purposes. In Moses' situation, he has good reason to be scared. He is being asked to go to Pharaoh, the tyrannical dictator of the most powerful nation on earth, and tell him to let his prime labor force go for no reason at all. No wonder Moses is afraid and ready to make a long list of excuses as to why this is a bad idea. As we look at the history of Israel, the good news is that God uses Moses to accomplish exactly what he says he will!

WORD STUDY: YAHWEH

The name *Yahweh* is used almost seven thousand times in the Old Testament. It was so revered by the Jewish people that they wouldn't even pronounce it. We don't even know the exact, correct pronunciation because they wouldn't say it out loud—they revered it so much.

Its significance here means that God is saying; "I'll make myself known to you." That's what names were all about back then. It is as if God is saying, "I'll reveal my character, my identity. I am the God who knows and sees and cares and acts. I am with you."

Questions 9–10

There are many parallels between the Passover story and the story of Jesus. It was John the Baptist who cried out when he saw Jesus, "Look, the Lamb of God, who takes away the sin of the world!" The apostle Paul made a direct connection when he wrote about this very connection (1 Corinthians 5:6–8). The fact that Jesus instituted the Lord's Supper in connection with the Passover meal ties the two even closer together (Matthew 26:17–30).

THE HEART
of a Leader

As we study Exodus, we discover that God makes us holy as we enter a living relationship with him. Yet, holiness is also something that continues growing in us for a lifetime. In this message we will hear the invitation of God to grow in holiness. One of the first steps to growing in holiness is identifying our need of God's cleansing. We need to identify the presence of sin in our hearts and lives and bring it before the holy God, who desires to wash us clean. As you prepare to lead your small group, read 1 John 1:8–10 and invite the Holy Spirit to begin searching your heart and revealing areas of hidden sin. Seek to lead your small group with a humble heart. Pray that you will become profoundly aware of your need to grow in holiness.

THE PRAYER
of a Leader

Take time, as you prepare to lead your small group, to meditate on the first half of Leviticus 11:44: "I am the LORD your God; consecrate yourselves and be holy, because I am holy." Pray for eyes to see the holiness of God. Ask God to let holiness grow in your life. Pray for a spirit of humility to invade the room where your small group meets. Also, pray for this same humility to go with them into their homes, workplace, and everywhere they go.

Question 1

The standard for hot dogs, fig paste, and even coffee is not nearly as pure as we think it should be. This is also true of our hearts. It's true of our words. It's true of our minds. It's true of our culture, media, and relationships. We live in an impure world.

Every human being alive convinces himself or herself that "my little impurities don't really matter. They don't really amount to much. They're really quite tolerable." But add them all up, and you have the tragedy of the world in which we live—the downward spiral of human sin.

Questions 2–4

In Exodus 19 we come to the foot of Mount Sinai. Here we see a ragtag group of frightened, grumbling, fugitive slaves. They have no real sense of identity yet and no clear knowledge of God. They are thoroughly impure. They are ready to run back to Egypt at the first sign of difficulty.

What is amazing is that God is banking his whole hope to redeem the world on these people. How can God possibly get them to appreciate how high the stakes are? What must he do to help them see that their little lives matter so much? God longs to help these people understand that there is another way to live besides the kind of grasping, clutching, grubbing, and grabbing they have grown accustomed to.

You can almost see this fearful group of wanderers standing in stunned amazement as they begin to realize that God is serious! His plan to impact and reach the whole world with his love will be built on this group of people. And, to accomplish this great purpose, this people will need to grow in holiness.

Questions 5–7

Something unique and important happened in Israel's understanding of holiness as time passed. The holiness that sets God apart came to be understood, above all else, as his moral excellence, his blinding purity, his perfect character. This God was set apart from sin.

Now here is the problem: This holy God is in relationship with this group of people at the foot of the mountain, and they are steeped in sin. He is also in relationship with us, and we are no less tainted by sin than the people we read about in Exodus. Since the Fall, every human being who has walked this earth (except Jesus) has been marked by sin, and this leads to a terrible ambivalence towards this holy God. We are drawn to holiness, we hunger for it, but we are afraid of it. We long for it, we know we need it, and yet we fear it will destroy us.

Questions 8–10

The Ten Commandments were given in the context of God's covenantal grace. This can be seen when we understand the nature of how ancient covenants were preserved. There was always a provision for preserving a copy of a covenant. This was done by making two copies of every covenant. Since there were no copy machines in those days, it was very costly to have each covenant draw up twice, but it was so important that they always did it. There was always a back-up copy so that the agreement would not be lost.

When Moses came down from the mountain with the Ten Commandments, he was carrying two tablets. Most people think that God ran out of space on the first tablet so he kept writing on a second one. Others have a picture in their mind of two tablets with five commandments on each. But the reason for the two tablets is that God provided a copy for each party (himself and the people) in accordance to the custom of the day. This way, the people of Israel could keep a copy and read and reread it publicly.

When we see the Ten Commandments, they are usually hanging on a wall, and they read like a list of do's and don'ts—a list of rules to be followed. The people of Israel would have looked at them differently. They saw a promise of the presence of God. They saw God's copy of his covenant with them. The very first line read, "I am the LORD *your* God." They carried both copies with them as a reminder of God's loving agreement to be in relationship with them. Were they expected to follow these commandments? Yes! But was God's love for them based on perfect obedience to these commands? No, for he had expressed and promised his love before these laws were given.

With all of this in mind, you can begin to get a picture of what it meant when Israel broke the commands of God. They were not just breeching some little agreement or bending some little rule. They were breaking their covenant with the God who loved them so passionately.

When Israel disobeyed God by making and worshiping the golden calf, do you remember how Moses responded? He smashed the tablets. He shattered them. This was not a thoughtless outburst of anger on his part. The tablets were the visible sign of the covenant. Moses was doing symbolically what the people were doing literally—*breaking the covenant.*

THE HEART
of a Leader

In this session you will look at four different life-lessons drawn from the wilderness time in the history of Israel. As you prepare to learn about these lessons with God's people, ask the Holy Spirit to speak to your heart about which lesson is for you today. Identify one key lesson that really hits home for you. How does this lesson affirm a positive direction you are moving in your journey toward God? Does it uncover ways you are wandering away from God's plan for your life? What adjustments can you make to align your life and attitudes more closely with God's plan for you?

THE PRAYER
of a Leader

God longs for us to learn from the lessons of those who have gone before us. Pray for the hearts of each of your group members to be soft enough to receive the unique message they need to hear. This session introduces four distinct lessons. Pray that the Holy Spirit will begin preparing each person to experience genuine transformation through this study.

Question 1

The wisest people learn from the examples of others. Sometimes the lessons learned show the path to life. At other times, these lessons show us which paths to avoid. As we look at the people of Israel in their wilderness wanderings, we learn from their victories and their failures. In this message God will invite us to grow in wisdom as we learn from those who have gone before us. Their pitfalls can be avoided. Their victories can be repeated. And we can grow as we walk through the wilderness experiences of our own lives.

God keeps his people in the wilderness because he has certain lessons they need to learn. The wilderness doesn't provide a lot of distractions. In the wilderness, people are a lot more likely to pay attention to God. It is a furnace where God can refine, melt, and purify his people and shape them into who he wants them to be. Throughout the history of the Old

Testament many of God's most important people spent time in the wilderness furnace: Moses, David, Elijah, and the people of Israel. God still invites those he loves to his wilderness school.

Questions 2–3

There is a huge spiritual lesson in the travel plans God has for Israel: He is not in a hurry! His primary concern is not speed. Ours usually is. God knows that *where* the people of Israel are going is not nearly as important as *who* they are becoming. God knows that possessing a land flowing with milk and honey is not nearly as important as having a heart flowing with love, justice, courage, and faith. God's first concern is not how fast his people get to the Promised Land; rather, his deepest concern is that they will be the right kind of people once they arrive. If it takes forty years to prepare their hearts, then so be it!

We have a certain way of looking at time. Our perspective is limited because we live within the confines of space and time. God has a radically different vantage point. He created time and space, and he is not subject to their limitations. This is why the apostle Peter writes, "But do not forget this one thing, dear friends: With the Lord a day is like a thousand years, and a thousand years are like a day" (2 Peter 3:8). We might be in a hurry, but God has a better view than we do; he created time, so we can trust him to lead us in his timing.

Questions 4–5

God has a long memory—he never forgets. We have short memories—we forget too easily. All through the history of Israel we see a pattern of setting up memorials as reminders of the great things God has done. Sometimes it is a pile of stones, at other times it is a special day of celebration or some other reminder. The key is that God wants his children to remember what he has done for them in the past so they can be certain that their future is in his hands.

Modern-day followers of God need to learn how to set up memorials. We also have short memories and are prone to spend much of our time looking forward at what we want God to do rather than looking back at everything he has done. God wants us to live with a balance. Looking forward and dreaming about the future are good and healthy! At the same time, reflecting about the past and celebrating what God has done is essential as well. We need to learn to keep one eye on the road ahead of us, but always have an eye to the past, celebrating all God has already done.

Questions 6-8

The people have grumbled and complained. They have become discontent and have begun to look back on the "glory days" of Egypt. We might expect God to get upset, impatient, or even angry, but he is very gracious. He just keeps providing. God gives the people meat in the form of quail and bread in the form of manna.

God's provision is wonderful. It is exactly what his people need, and there is enough for everyone. Every day, one day at a time, God gives what they need. In an interesting twist, we learn that anytime the people gather more than they need and try to stockpile it for the next day, the food goes rotten and is filled with maggots. They can only gather what they need for the day. Then, to the amazement of all the people, when they gather twice as much as they need on the day before the Sabbath (as God commanded), the manna stays fresh.

Questions 9-10

Moses sends out twelve spies, and they are gone for forty days. They come back and file their report. Look at Numbers 13:27: "They gave Moses this account: 'We went into the land to which you sent us, and it does flow with milk and honey!'" It's a land of abundance.

The spies are clear that the reports of the amazing bounty of this land are not exaggerated. But they also point out that the people who live there are big and strong. The cities are fortified. They want Moses and all of the people to know that this is a dangerous place. Ten of the spies bring a bad report and discourage the people from even trying to go in and take the land.

Then two of the spies, Joshua and Caleb, give a dissenting report. Numbers 13:30 says: "Then Caleb silenced the people before Moses and said, 'We should go up and take possession of the land, for we can certainly do it.'" But the people in the wilderness school don't believe this. They don't believe that God's protection will be enough for them. They refuse to enter. What a sobering reality the people of Israel face. The negative spirit of a few people poison a whole community. What a reminder that walking in faith, not in fear, is God's plan for his followers.

What Indiana Jones Was Looking For

THE HEART
of a Leader

You can tell a lot about a person by where he or she lives. If you get a chance to visit someone's home and do a brief walk-through, you can gain great insight to their values, loves, and priorities. For better or for worse, we make pretty strong judgments and decisions about a person based on the environment they live in.

In this message we will look at the house of God. In the Pentateuch we learn about God's choice to dwell among his people. His dwelling place, the tabernacle, gives us amazing insight to his heart and how he relates with his children.

As you prepare to lead this small group, take time to walk around your home and reflect on what you see. What do you learn about your values, priorities, and passions? Let this experience help shape how you look at the passages in this week's message. The tabernacle, with all its furnishings, points to God's values, priorities, and passions. After you have surveyed your own home and God's dwelling place as shown in these passages, think about how you might change the furnishing in your home (literally or spiritually) to line up your life more closely with God's priorities for you.

THE PRAYER
of a Leader

As you prepare to lead this group, lift up two simple but life-changing prayers. First, pray for each of your small-group members, including you, to grow in a deeper awareness of God's presence with them every moment of every day. Second, pray that each of your group members will begin to organize their lives around God rather than around the other things that clamor for our attention.

LEADER'S NOTES

115

Questions 2–4

The presence of the tabernacle in the middle of the camp of Israel is a picture of God's message to Moses that the people need a physical reminder that he is with them. They need a place full of details and activities that will teach them about God's character and will, and about how they can relate to him. God says, "I will come and meet with you on top of that box, I will provide manna for you every morning, and I will give you water to drink. I will lead you through the desert from one river to another." And the God of the universe says, "I will live in a tent out in the desert just so I can be with my people." All this detail, all the instructions, are given so that the people can have a place to meet with their God.

The word "dwell" (Exodus 25:8) has a specific meaning. In the Hebrew language it is the same root word as the one used for a tabernacle. It's a little like our modern word "tent." Literally, Exodus 25:8 can be translated as God saying, "I will tabernacle with my people." In other words, this is not just the word used for a *place* (the tent) in the middle of the camp of Israel. It is also the word that describes what God *is doing*. His activity was, and is, to tabernacle (dwell) among his people.

As we study the tabernacle, we are really studying how we can learn to dwell with God. The tabernacle gives powerful insight and instruction that helps us learn to enter a new and rich relationship with our Creator. As we begin to walk through the tabernacle toward the dwelling place of God, we need to realize that our attitude and heart condition influence the process.

Questions 5–7

THE BRONZE ALTAR

The sacrifices of the people took place every day, and this altar is the place these sacrifices were offered. They were brought the first thing in the morning and the last thing at night. The priests offered sacrifices for individuals, for families, and for the nation. This altar is the picture the apostle Paul had in mind in Romans 12:1 when he writes, "Offer your body as a living sacrifice."

The picture would have been clear in the minds of the Israelites. When an animal was to be sacrificed, it was tied to the horns that were on the corners of the altar. The animal didn't have the option to say, "Well, I think I'm done now. I'm going to get up and leave." It was tied to the altar, and there was no way off the altar except through death. Paul's words in Romans 12 express utter surrender and submission. Like the animal tied to the altar, we are bound to give our whole lives in sacrifice to the God who sacrificed all for us.

The entire sacrificial system, which was detailed and complex, pointed forward to a final sacrifice that would be offered for sins. One day Jesus would become the perfect sacrifice. Until then, the sacrificial system reminded people of the cost of sin and the hope of cleansing and restored relationship with God.

THE BASIN

In Bible times the people didn't have a chance to get cleaned up very often, and giving an opportunity for washing was an act of gracious hospitality. In the tabernacle a large part of what the priests did was to butcher animals. That's a messy job. In Exodus 30:17 we learn that the basin was placed between the altar and the Tent of Meeting so that when the priests entered God's presence, they cleansed themselves first "so that they would not die" (see Exodus 30:20).

Again, this is a picture of what it was to be clean in God's sight. This cleansing was not just for the body, not just for the clothes, but for the conscience. The vision was that people would realize that God offers purity. Imagine a heart with no stain, no regret, and no remorse.

We live in a world that is unclean. We can feel the grit and grime of the world cling to our minds and souls. Yet God still offers cleansing. He offers purity of heart, even for the greatest of sinners. As we look into the water of the bronze basin, we see a reflection—we see ourselves. We see our sin, our offense, our hopelessness. But as we plunge beneath the water, we are reminded that God has the power to cleanse. Jesus offers to make us white as snow if we will receive his cleansing.

THE LAMPSTAND

Inside the tabernacle was an outer chamber called the Holy Place. In an ancient Near Eastern home there was a place where you would receive a guest and perhaps break bread. In the tabernacle there were three main pieces of furniture in the Holy Place, similar to common furnishings in homes at that time. There was a lampstand, burning incense, and fresh bread.

The lampstand stood as an ever-present reminder that God is the One who brings light in the darkness. God said to his priests, "Don't let the lamp go out. I want all my people to know that when they're confused, when they're afraid, when they're in the dark, I'll leave the light on. I am here. I am available to them all day and all night."

THE ALTAR OF INCENSE

In the tabernacle was a simple reminder that God desires to hear our prayers. The book of Revelation teaches us that our prayers ascend to the throne of God like sweet incense. What a beautiful picture! As you think of the altar of incense, remember that God longs to hear your prayers. Let this be a reminder of his invitation for you to enter his presence any time of any day!

THE BREAD OF THE PRESENCE

Breaking bread and sharing table fellowship (a meal) with others was important in Bible days. Today we tend to sit down for a meal only with people we know and like. But in those days there was deep meaning in sharing a meal and breaking bread, even with strangers. When you broke bread, you were entering a level of intimate fellowship much deeper than what we express through a shared meal in our culture today.

This is why the religious leaders of Jesus' day were so outraged when Jesus, a rabbi, actually broke bread with sinners. He was entering an intimate experience with people who were to be avoided, according to the religious laws of the day. In the days of Moses, everyone knew that breaking bread and sharing table fellowship was a sign of deep intimacy. With that in mind, the idea that God would have bread prepared for his people spoke volumes about his desire to be close to his people.

Questions 8–10

One way God invited his people to come near to him was through simple reminders. In the ark, God had the high priest place some objects that would always be there to help remind the people that they were welcome to come near to him. First, there was a bowl of manna. This was a reminder that God would always be faithful and provide, one day at a time.

Next was Aaron's rod. The people knew the story (from the book of Numbers) about how God miraculously caused Aaron's rod to bud in order to inform all the Israelites that Aaron and his descendents were to be God's priests to lead them in worship. The rod of Aaron reminded them that God invites his people to come and worship. Also, it served as a warning from God. The people had grumbled often in the wilderness (the opposite of worship). God wanted them to realize that grumbling was a sin and that their intimacy with God and worship would be hindered if they did not get this under control.

Finally, God told the people to put the two tablets that contained the Ten Commandments into the box. This was the people's copy and God's copy of the covenant. It was God's reminder that they were to draw near to him with obedient hearts.

Each item in the ark, therefore, taught a lesson from God for his people:

- Manna—trust me
- The rod of Aaron—worship me and beware of grumbling
- The tablets of the Ten Commandments—obey me

Trust, worship, and obedience represent the heart of what it means to live with God. The objects in the ark became symbols and reminders of God's desire for intimacy with his people.

LEADER'S NOTES

THE HEART
of a Leader

Jesus said, "For where your treasure is, there your heart will be also" (Matthew 6:21). We live in a world that invites us to fall in love with something new every day. New products, new hobbies, new culinary sensations, and new entertainments cry out for our attention. In the midst of this cacophony of voices, God speaks to us and invites us to love his law. He does not scream his invitation; rather, he simply sets before us the richness of his law and invites us to hear, learn, and grow to cherish the words of life and truth that have been loved by his people for millennia.

How would you describe your love for God's law? Does it fill your mind? Do you find yourself hungering to know God's law in deeper ways? As you prepare to lead this small-group study, meditate on the goodness of God's law. Consider taking time to read Psalm 119 slowly and in its entirety. This psalm celebrates God's law in a way that will draw you in and invite you to see it in new and fresh ways. As you read, reflect on the following questions:

- When was a time that I really fell deeper in love with God's Word?
- What life experiences draw me deeper into God's Word?
- What can I do to make the personal study of Scripture a bigger priority in my life?

THE PRAYER
of a Leader

Begin praying that your heart will fall deeper and deeper in love with God through his Word. Ask God to help you establish a lifelong discipline of reading his Word even after you finish reading through the Old Testament. Pray for each of your small-group members to grow in their love for the Word of God through this study.

Question 1

The Law was so prized that the people were to keep their eyes focused on it at all times. They were to hold tightly to God's teachings so they would not slip through their fingers, out of their hearts, and get lost. This is an interesting image in light of the fact that later in their history, the people of Israel lost focus and let their grasp on the Law slip, and it was lost. In the days of kings of Israel, there was a season in time when the book of the law of God was lost (literally); it was finally found again in the days of Josiah (2 Kings 22:1–13).

To get a sense of how the people cherished the Law, read these verses:

> *[The ordinances of the Lord] are more precious than gold,*
>   *than much pure gold;*
> *they are sweeter than honey,*
>   *than honey from the comb. (Psalm 19:10)*
>
> *Oh, how I love your law!*
>   *I meditate on it all day long. (Psalm 119:97)*
>
> *Your statutes are my heritage forever;*
>   *they are the joy of my heart. (Psalm 119:111)*

The wisest people living in Israel loved God's law with all their hearts. We don't think about the law much in our day. We certainly don't love and cherish it. It is unlikely that many of us meditate on the legal code of our city or state. We don't love our law that way. But the people of Israel saw their law as the greatest source of wisdom the world had ever seen.

Questions 2–4

Gleaning laws: When God called the people to leave some of the harvest in the field, they knew that they could have gone over the fields twice and beat the olive trees a little harder to be sure everything fell to the ground and could be taken to the market for a profit. They could have brought in a bigger harvest, made a better profit, and gotten a better return on their investment. But God called them to be sloppy and always leave some in their fields. Why? Because something inside the human heart tends to say, "I've got to wring every ounce of profit out of this I can. I've got to make every dime I can grab." To counteract this selfish tendency, God instituted the gleaning laws.

The year of Jubilee: This is a powerful picture in the Old Testament. When Jesus came, he used Jubilee language to describe the era he inaugurated. The year of Jubilee was a time when freedom came for all people. To prevent chronic poverty, God said, "Every fifty years, all the land is to go back to its original owner." This was a radical redistribution of the wealth, where everyone got back their family inheritance that had been established in the days of Joshua.

The goal of the Old Testament laws was never to make us mechanical in our responses. In Deuteronomy 15:7–8 we read, "If there is a poor man among your brothers in any of the towns of the land that the LORD your God is giving you, do not be hardhearted or tightfisted toward your poor brother. Rather be openhanded and freely lend him whatever he needs." Imagine a community where everybody is joyfully openhanded with what they have. Think about what a community of people could be like if they make their resources available to God, to the people of God, and to those who are in need. We need to ask ourselves how we can grow in generosity and keep our hands open and our resources available.

In the book of Acts we see this dream of sacrificial generosity lived out in the early church. The Holy Spirit descends, hearts are changed, and people begin to live with an openhanded and giving attitude: "All the believers were together and had everything in common. Selling their possessions and goods, they gave to anyone as he had need" (Acts 2:44–45).

Questions 5–7

Many people think the Old Testament is the story of a dark, grim God overseeing a scared and somber people. It is not so. God calls his people to be holy: "Be holy as I am holy"—which means to be set apart. One of the ways his people were to be holy, unique, and set apart was for them to be joyful. The feasts are reminders, training exercises, for us to grow in joy. Many people have trouble being joyful, but God is ready to help them grow in joy.

We can't miss the reality that God is filled with passionate joy and that he calls his children to lives of committed celebration. The book of Deuteronomy recounts God's call for his people to gather for festivals and times of joy-filled remembrance. In Deuteronomy we hear the invitation to live as people who regularly celebrate the goodness of our God.

Two words come up again and again when these feasts and remembrances are commanded in the Pentateuch: *celebrate* and *rejoice*. God is deeply concerned that we grow as a people of joy. He wants, he commands, us to celebrate his great works and amazing provision. In Deuteronomy 16:14 the people are told to, "Be joyful at your feasts." What a great reminder!

Notice God's concern for including everyone in the celebration (Deuteronomy 16:1–12). The religious leaders, who have no land as their possession, are called to be part of the festival. The immigrants, widows, and orphans are also to be included. They are to be invited, and provision is to be made for them.

God still wants his followers to invite others to join in our celebrations. From church services to backyard BBQs on holidays, God wants us to invite others to share in the joy. Our joyous celebrations speak volumes to a world that looks on and wonders if our faith is real. Each time we are getting ready for some kind of celebration, why not ask ourselves: *Are there people I know who need a little joy in their lives? Whom might I invite to a special church event, a party, or some gathering where Christ's followers are going to be celebrating life?* We can learn to include others in our modern-day festivals and watch what happens as they are swept into the joy of God and his people.

Questions 8–10

In the ancient world, the world in which Moses lived, people with power took whatever vengeance they wanted on somebody who hurt them. If someone was hurt a little bit, they could hurt back a lot. Not only that, but they would even inflict punishment on the next of kin. If they couldn't get at the perpetrator, they would attack and punish a son, daughter, spouse, or even extended family and friends. This disproportionate punishment was common practice. It was considered acceptable.

In light of this, when Moses wrote, "Eye for an eye, tooth for a tooth," it was not encouraging vengeance; it was *limiting it.* This law was intended to restrain vengeance. It taught that evil must be punished, but the punishment must be proportionate, not disproportionate. In light of where people were at this time in history, the people would have understood that this law was given to discourage violence, not to encourage it.

Willow Creek Association
Vision, Training, Resources for Prevailing Churches

This resource was created to serve you and to help you in building a local church that prevails!
Since 1992, the Willow Creek Association (WCA) has been linking like-minded, action-oriented churches with each other and with strategic vision, training, and resources. Now a worldwide network of over 6,400 churches from more than ninety denominations, the WCA works to equip Member Churches and others with the tools needed to build prevailing churches. Our desire is to inspire, equip, and encourage Christian leaders to build biblically functioning churches that reach increasing numbers of unchurched people, not just with innovations from Willow Creek Community Church in South Barrington, Illinois, but from any church in the world that has experienced God-given breakthroughs.

WILLOW CREEK CONFERENCES
Each year, thousands of local church leaders, staff and volunteers—from WCA Member Churches and others—attend one of our conferences or training events. Conferences offered on the Willow Creek campus in South Barrington, Illinois, include:

Prevailing Church Conference: Foundational training for staff and volunteers working to build a prevailing local church.

Prevailing Church Workshops: More than fifty strategic, day-long workshops covering seven topic areas that represent key characteristics of a prevailing church; offered twice each year.

Promiseland Conference: Children's ministries; infant through fifth grade.

Student Ministries Conference: Junior and senior high ministries.

Willow Creek Arts Conference: Vision and training for Christian artists using their gifts in the ministries of local churches.

Leadership Summit: Envisioning and equipping Christians with leadership gifts and responsibilities; broadcast live via satellite to eighteen cities across North America.

Contagious Evangelism Conference: Encouragement and training for churches and church leaders who want to be strategic in reaching lost people for Christ.

Small Groups Conference: Exploring how developing a church *of* small groups can play a vital role in developing authentic Christian community that leads to spiritual transformation.

To find out more about WCA conferences, visit our website at www.willowcreek.com.

PREVAILING CHURCH REGIONAL WORKSHOPS
Each year the WCA team leads several, two-day training events in select cities across the United States. Some twenty day-long workshops are offered in topic areas including leadership, next-

generation ministries, small groups, arts and worship, evangelism, spiritual gifts, financial stewardship, and spiritual formation. These events make quality training more accessible and affordable to larger groups of staff and volunteers.

To find out more about Prevailing Church Regional Workshops, visit our website at www.willowcreek.com.

Willow Creek Resources™

Churches can look to Willow Creek Resources™ for a trusted channel of ministry tools in areas of leadership, evangelism, spiritual gifts, small groups, drama, contemporary music, financial stewardship, spiritual transformation, and more. For ordering information, call (800) 570-9812 or visit our website at www.willowcreek.com.

WCA Membership

Membership in the Willow Creek Association as well as attendance at WCA Conferences is for churches, ministries, and leaders who hold to a historic, orthodox understanding of biblical Christianity. The annual church membership fee of $249 provides substantial discounts for your entire team on all conferences and Willow Creek Resources, networking opportunities with other outreach-oriented churches, a bimonthly newsletter, a subscription to the *Defining Moments* monthly audio journal for leaders, and more.

To find out more about WCA membership, visit our website at www.willowcreek.com.

WillowNet (www.willowcreek.com)

This Internet resource service provides access to hundreds of Willow Creek messages, drama scripts, songs, videos, and multimedia ideas. The system allows you to sort through these elements and download them for a fee.

Our website also provides detailed information on the Willow Creek Association, Willow Creek Community Church, WCA membership, conferences, training events, resources, and more.

WillowCharts.com (www.willowcharts.com)

Designed for local church worship leaders and musicians, WillowCharts.com provides online access to hundreds of music charts and chart components, including choir, orchestral, and horn sections, as well as rehearsal tracks and video streaming of Willow Creek Community Church performances.

The NET (http://studentministry.willowcreek.com)

The NET is an online training and resource center designed by and for student ministry leaders. It provides an inside look at the structure, vision, and mission of prevailing student ministries from around the world. The NET gives leaders access to complete programming elements, including message outlines, dramas, small group questions, and more. An indispensable resource and networking tool for prevailing student ministry leaders!

Contact the Willow Creek Association

If you have comments or questions, or would like to find out more about WCA events or resources, please contact us:

Willow Creek Association
P.O. Box 3188, Barrington, IL 60011-3188
Phone: (800) 570-9812 or (847) 765-0070
Fax (888) 922-0035 or (847) 765-5046
Web: www.willowcreek.com

DISCOVER THE LIFE-CHANGING RELEVANCE OF THE OLD TESTAMENT

Pressed for time? Check out the special "Fast Track" reading guide!

Taking the Old Testament Challenge
Judson Poling

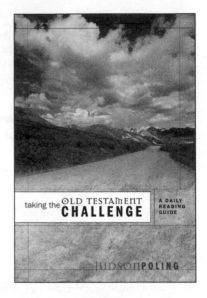

If you've ever . . .

- wondered what's in the Bible Jesus studied
- promised yourself, "One of these days, I'm going to get serious about reading the whole Old Testament"
- wanted a personal "guide" to lead you through unfamiliar territory in the Old Testament

. . . then this book is for you!

In less than a year, you can travel through the entire Old Testament from Genesis to Malachi. These daily readings, comments, and questions will deepen your walk with God and heighten your knowledge of his Word. But this book is far more than a simple reading program, it will lead you to a devotional experience with God.

Discover why Jesus was so passionate about the Old Testament and quoted from it so frequently. As you open this reading guide and your Bible, you'll see why the same ancient wisdom that Jesus treasured is just what you need for your life today.

Taking the Old Testament Challenge is an integral part of the Old Testament Challenge, a dynamic program for churches. This individual reading guide brings the Old Testament up close and personal as each participant takes a life-transforming journey through the first two-thirds of the Bible. The truths of Scripture will enter deep into hearts and lives—with applications that turn lessons into lifestyles and principles into practice.

Softcover: 0-310-24913-9

Pick up a copy today at your favorite bookstore!

ZONDERVAN™

GRAND RAPIDS, MICHIGAN 49530 USA

WWW.ZONDERVAN.COM

AN A–Z TOUR
OLD TESTAMENT CHALLENGE

Implementation Guide
Discover the Life-Changing Relevance of the Old Testament

Kevin Harney and Mindy Caliguire

The *Implementation Guide* gives aid on how to lead a comprehensive tour through the Old Testament Challenge experience. It is an A–Z overview of the full program, giving leaders all the tools they will need to rally church support, build a leadership team, prepare for the Old Testament Challenge, launch the OTC, lead the thirty-two-week Old Testament program on three interlocking levels (congregation wide, small groups, and individual), and end the Old Testament Challenge in a way that will propel church members forward with a new passion and commitment to God's Word. Through using this guide, the Old Testament Challenge will be an experience your congregation will never forget.

The OTC offers a great benefit to those who take the challenge. At our church, we often found that people suffered from "spiritual information overload." They would hear one talk at a weekend service, another during our mid-week worship time; they would discuss a third topic in their small group and look at a fourth one in their personal reading. It was like drinking from a fire hydrant. The OTC has a revolutionary impact on spiritual growth because it weds together a teaching experience, small group learning, and individual study all around one weekly theme! This guide will give you a road map to lead your congregation on a life-transforming journey through the Old Testament.
– John Ortberg

Softcover: 0-310-24939-2

Pick up a copy today at your favorite bookstore!

ZONDERVAN™

GRAND RAPIDS, MICHIGAN 49530 USA

WWW.ZONDERVAN.COM

OLD TESTAMENT CHALLENGE
Discover the Life-Changing Relevance of the Old Testament

Teaching Guide
John Ortberg with
Kevin and Sherry Harney

Preaching and teaching God's Word is one of the most intense joys in this life. It is also one of the greatest challenges! In our media-driven, fast-paced, sensory-intensive culture, where can you find the resources needed to communicate the age-old message of the Old Testament in a way that awakens this generation to the voice of God? Where do you find the historical, cultural, and geographical background on a passage that will transport the listeners thousands of years into the past so they can see, hear, smell, taste, and touch the ancient world? Where can you look to find illustrations, humorous stories, and word pictures that will rivet the message of the Old Testament to the hearts of listeners in a way they will never forget? Where can you go to find creative ways to apply the lessons of the Old Testament in a way that will bring undeniable transformation?

This teacher's resource guide is the answer to each of these questions. The genius of this teacher's guide is that it gives you the freedom to create your own message from a treasury of resources. It provides room for you to add your unique contribution so that each message bears your distinct teaching DNA in a way that naturally fits your unique context. This revolutionary tool provides up to sixteen categories of material for each message so that you do not have to spend countless hours digging and hunting, but you will begin your preparation with a wealth of ideas and resources!

This Teacher's resource includes the following tools for message preparation:

- Creative Message Ideas
- Heart of the Message
- Heart of the Messenger
- Historical Context Notes
- Illustrations
- Interpretive Insights
- Life Applications
- Narrative on Life
- Narrative on the Text
- New Testament Connections
- On the Lighter Side
- Pause for Prayer
- Pause for Reflections
- Quotable Quotes
- Significant Scriptures
- Word Studies

Softcover: 0-310-24892-2